AF411533

ZOOM/TPU
INTERIOR DESIGN FROM ISTANBUL

Philip Jodidio

PRESTEL
Munich · London · New York

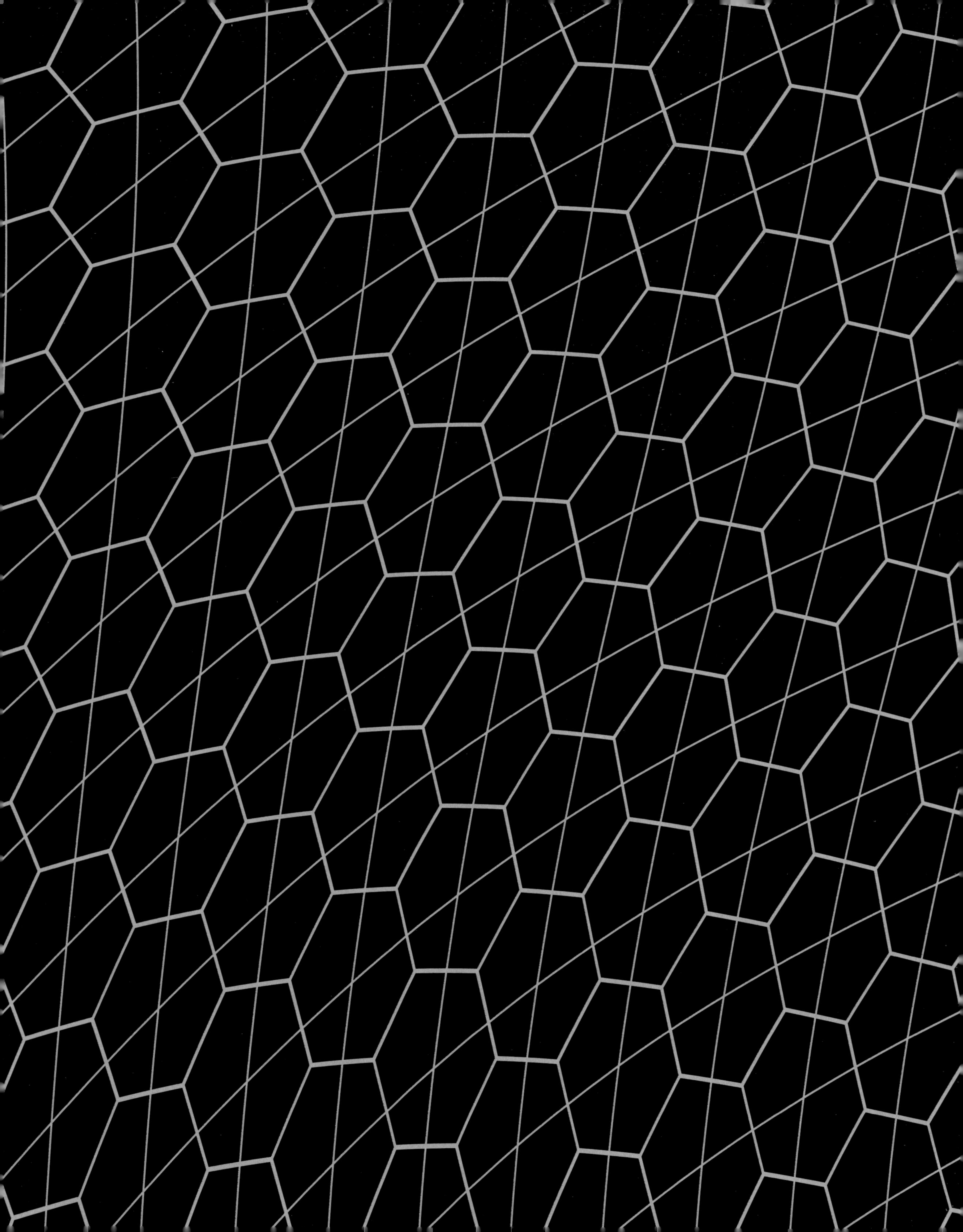

Contents

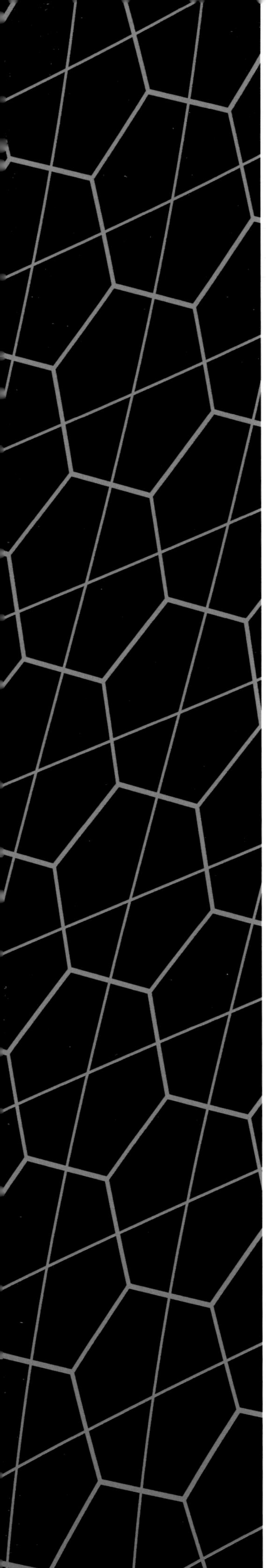

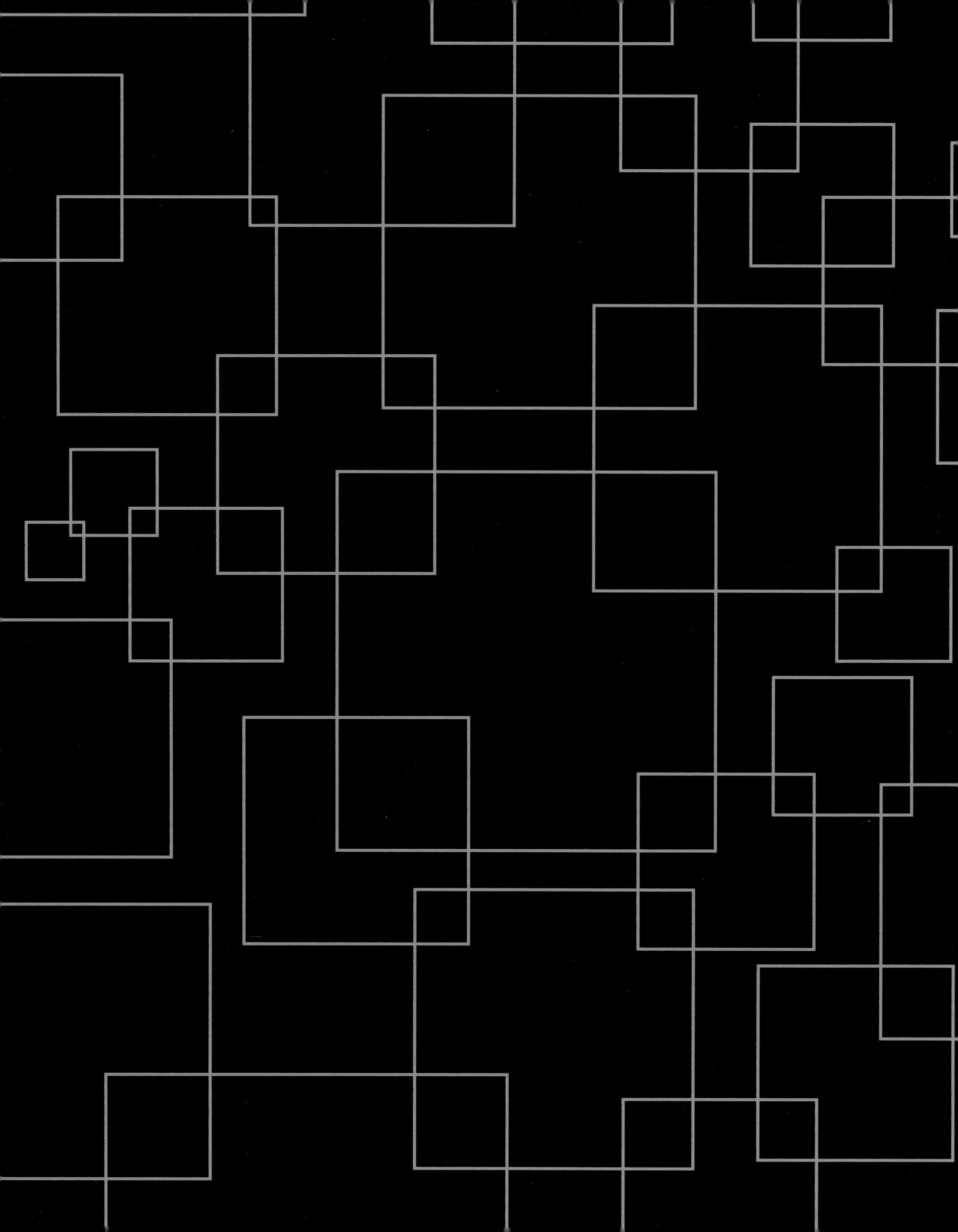

Preface

We have been hoping to create this book ever since we first established Zoom/TPU.

While we were still at school, we both believed in the power of "printed matter." Fundamentally we imagined that anything printed can be considered important. This idea has been supported by our experience on many occasions; that is why we have always given value to the catalogues that we have published regularly about our work.

When we gave our latest catalogue to Professor Dr. Celal Abdi Guzer of the Middle East Technical University he was kind enough to say: "This is a catalogue that looks like it wishes to become a book." After that, we saw that the Turkish architects Murat and Melkan Tabanlioglu,[1] Emre Arolat[2] and Ali Osman Ozturk[3] had produced their own books with international publishers, which impressed us and gave us courage. We decided to publish our first book outside of Turkey because we feel that we are ready to go beyond our own borders. We live in a wonderfully rich, historic, architectural environment, but unfortunately too little has been preserved. The same may apply to professional values in Turkey, which is also why we are ready to travel and to learn.

Our focus has been on interior design projects, but, here, we wanted to share our interior design, architecture, and product design experiences and skills, to share the results of working together as an architect (Levent Cirpici) and an interior architect (Atilla Kuzu). Neither one of us comes from families of architects; we have traced our own route and learned as we have advanced. This situation has both advantages and disadvantages, but, above all, we are ready to go further.

We also wish to explain our work to an international audience, as well as to continue our existing presence in the local context. Our goal is to share our way of handling a variety of issues that we

Top: Atilla Kuzu
Bottom: Levent Cirpici

have faced with interior and architecture projects of differing scale and purpose, and the process of managing this work. We hope to open new horizons to those who find our work interesting, but also to be responsive to those who wish to provide us with their own opinions.

We are very thankful to those who have valued our work, experiences and these processes. Naturally, our projects have been carried out with our valued clients, client representatives, contractors, partners, and, of course, our co-workers, who have shared the excitement of each project with us. We can never thank those who have made our work possible enough.

Atilla Kuzu + Levent Cirpici, Istanbul, Turkey, 23 September 2014

1 Philip Jodidio, Suha Ozkan,
   *Tabanlioglu Architects:
   Transparency and Modernity*,
   Skira Rizzoli, New York, 2014.

2 Philip Jodidio, Suha Ozkan,
   *EAA Emre Arolat Architects:
   Context and Plurality*,
   Rizzoli, New York, 2013.

3 A. Tasarim Mimarlik:
   *The Architecture of Ali Osman
   Ozturk*, Images Publishing,
   Melbourne, 2014.

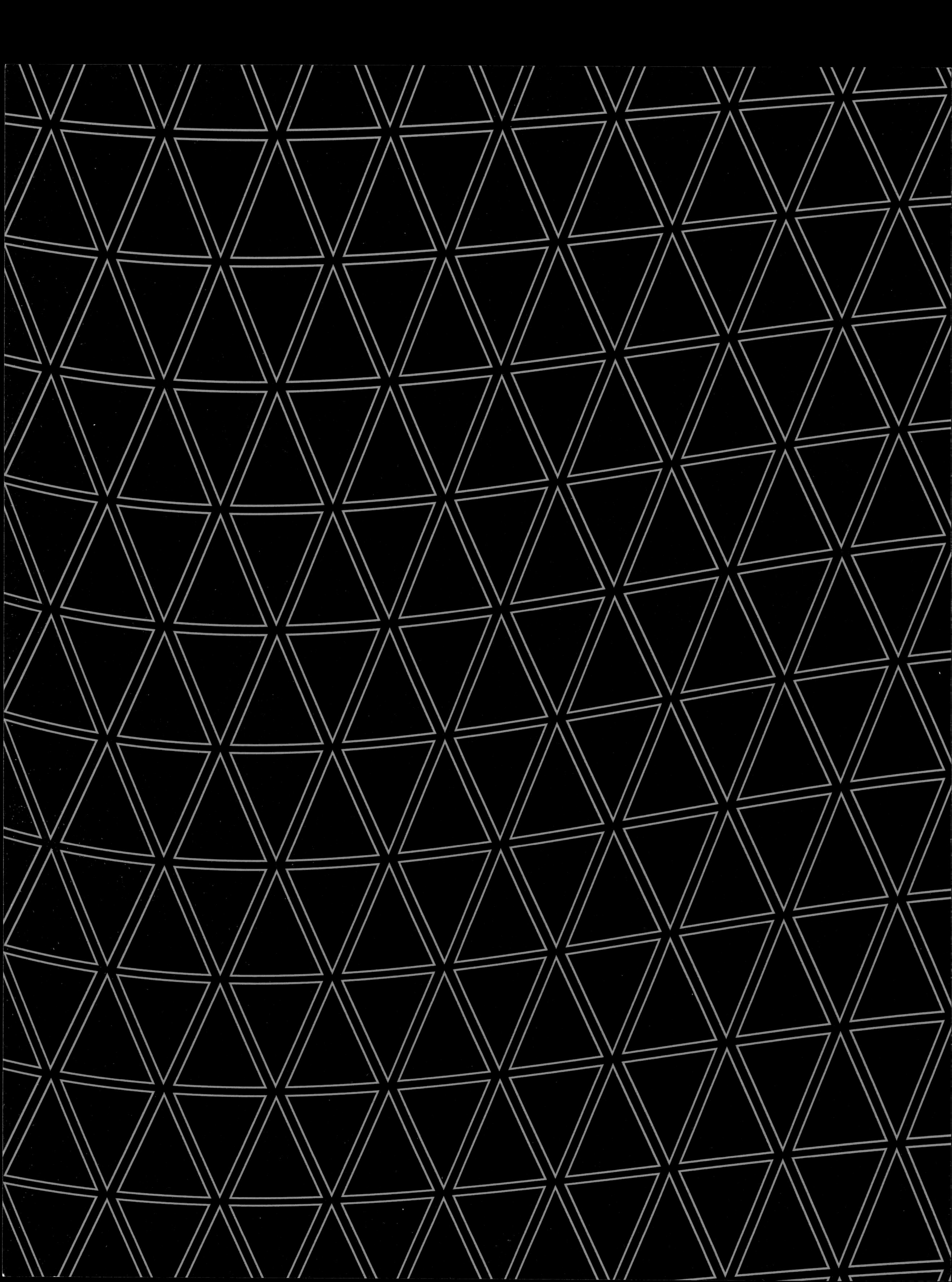

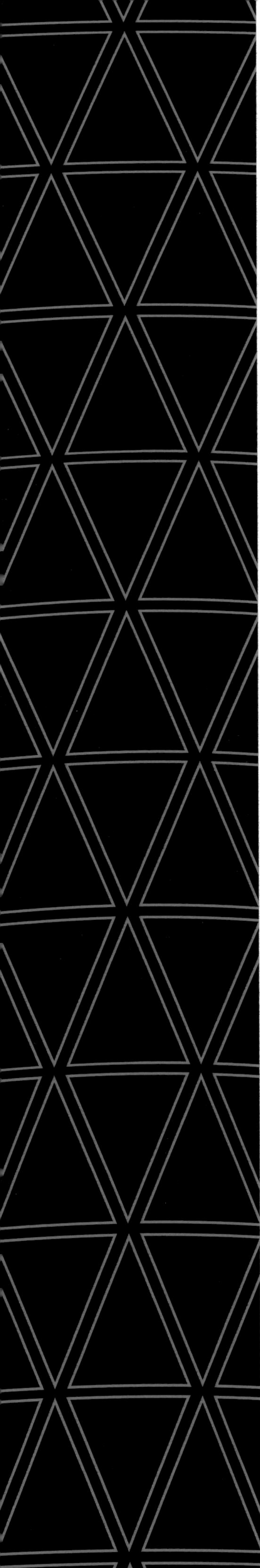

A Language of Forms
The Work of Zoom/TPU
by Philip Jodidio

Atilla Kuzu and Levent Cirpici cofounded the design and architecture office Zoom/TPU in Istanbul in 1994. The team has gained considerable notoriety in Turkey working on retail, health care, office buildings, housing, and congress centers. Their firm employs a number of architects and interior designers, and is located in the Siraselviler area of the historic Beyoglu/Taksim district of Istanbul. Atilla Kuzu, born in Istanbul in 1963, is an interior architect, although he originally hoped to be a doctor. He graduated from Marmara Fine Arts University (Istanbul, 1987). Levent Cirpici was born in 1965, in Erzurum, eastern Turkey, and graduated from the Faculty of Architecture at Mimar Sinan University in Istanbul in 1989. Like his partner, he imagined another career for himself, as a scientist. It might be said that, having wanted respectively to be a doctor and a scientist, the partners of Zoom/TPU have gone on to reflect their early interests in the work that they do even today. In particular, they have made a name for themselves in the area of hospital design. Prior to graduation, Levent Cirpici worked in the office of Professor Utarit Izgi (1983–87). His career as an architect advanced quickly and Levent Cirpici won second prize in the Sedat Gurel Dalyankoy Museum and Library Project Competition in 2000. The Figen and Servet Yazici Residence (Antalya, Turkey, 1999) by Cirpici and Kuzu was nominated for the 2001 Cycle of the Aga Khan Award for Architecture. Zoom/TPU was later part of a prestigious team of Turkish designers and architects responsible for the renovation of the SALT Galata project (Istanbul, Turkey, 2009–11), a former bank building that now houses a museum, an exhibition space for art, an open archive for research, a library, an auditorium (by Zoom/TPU; page 121), workshops, a restaurant, and office space. These are just two examples amongst many others of the outstanding design work of Zoom/TPU. This book constitutes the first, well-deserved, international exposure for these talented

designers, who have notably completed several major hospital commissions, confirming that good design and health care most definitely share a common goal, making people feel better.

A Fluid Design Process

The partners of Zoom/TPU have defined their own design approach as follows: "Our primary consideration in the design process is to perceive everything that is being transmitted to us by our clients fully and correctly; and combining this with the data relating to the space and the time expectations of our customers. Our work is thus the result of a fluid design process. However, like all other designers and architects, we are sometimes confronted with customers who insist on directing our design process. In these cases, we try to explain the essential elements of our design and to make the clients understand these considerations as much as we can. Our main goal in our work is not to be concentrated only on one subject. The economic rises and falls of Turkey generate profound changes in different work areas at different times which has also naturally been reflected on our careers. In 2005, when we started hospital projects, clients trusted our experience, which was based on one hospital at that time. By 2009, we were winning numerous awards for our hospital projects. Similarly, the Istanbul Lutfi Kirdar International Convention and Exhibition Center project was also one of our first experiences in that field, even though it was completed in a very limited time frame. Clearly we have transformed a number of 'first' efforts into successful lines of design, and our office philosophy is to always remain open to new projects that we will engage on with our twenty years of experience."

From Asia to Europe

Atilla Kuzu was working in the Istanbul office of the architect Hasan

Mingu in 1989 when Levent Cirpici joined the team. After working well together for five years and beginning to receive direct requests from some clients, they decided to start up their own firm. Their first office was located at Yogurtcu Parki on the Anatolian side of Istanbul, in a space of less than forty square meters. They started with a single employee, but had five after just two months of collaboration. In 1995, they moved their office to Kismet Palas at Moda, also in the Asian part of the city. Their first interior design projects were for a retail store, a branch bank's general management flat, and a shopping mall. Despite economic difficulties in Turkey in 1994, their practice continued to grow until 1998, when they again moved to larger quarters on Bagdat Avenue, a noted shopping street also on the Anatolian side. Finally, in 2012, the practice moved to Siraselviler Street in the historic Beyoglu/Taksim area on the European side of Istanbul. This is the office that is presented on page 171 of this book.

The name Zoom/TPU actually offers a full description of the work of the firm since they attempt to "zoom in," focusing on details of their work, ranging from construction plans to custom-designed furniture. TPU refers to "Tasarim Proje Uygulama" in Turkish, which means "Design Project Implementation." It is clear that unlike some architects and designers who content themselves with providing a general "sketch" or outline of a project, Zoom/TPU takes a much more "holistic" approach, looking closely into the needs of their clients and examining the details of materials and forms, following right through to realizations that have a very contemporary "seamless" feeling about them.

Atilla Kuzu and Levent Cirpici have never made a distinction between their respective professions—as an interior designer and an architect. Rather, they have worked as a team, handling architecture, interior design, and object design simultaneously. In fact, their different backgrounds have allowed them to adapt an interdisciplinary approach, crossing over barriers that normally separate professions, in particular where architecture and interior design are concerned. As the projects published here demonstrate, they have succeeded in creating their own language, and quite obviously in enjoying their work, the main reason for which the partnership has lasted twenty years.

Changing and Developing

Although the work of Zoom/TPU has been focused on Turkey and Istanbul in particular, the partners do not feel that their projects have a particularly "Turkish" style, even rejecting such an emphasis because they feel it is inappropriate for the kind of work they do. As they say: "Architecture may have its own language, but should not have a nationality." Although it differs from a majority of their projects, the 1300-square-meter Figen and Servet Yazici Residence (Antalya, Turkey), designed in 1999, marked an early milestone in their career. The two-story, white, stone-clad residence is characterized by open spaces and transparent façades. Located in a ten-hectare orange grove bordered by irrigation canals on two sides, the house was shortlisted for the 2001 Aga Khan Award for Architecture. It is sited not far from the city-center of Antalya. The architects speak of a "modern Mediterranean approach" in their design. Careful attention was paid to the placement of wide, vertical windows and skylights, according to local lighting conditions. Natural air circulation was preferred to mechanical air-conditioning. The house includes a covered swimming pool, spa, and a children's hobby room. The "public" areas of the house were planned so that they could maintain a "private" feel and yet bring together the owners, children, and guests. The pool and barbecue areas are placed in the large, green, flat spaces near the house.

One project that may have a more archeological or "Turkish" feeling to it is the Tiara Jewellery showroom located near the Grand

The design of the Tiara Jewellery showroom refers to the historic fabric of the area.

Bazaar in Istanbul (see page 95). Their reasoning in this instance is related to the fact that the brand itself and its location in a historic setting plead in favor of emphasizing "Turkish" qualities in the design.

Zoom/TPU has indeed sought to develop a characteristic style, but they deal with each project differently, clearly attempting to develop different solutions for each project. They seek to develop their own language, adding to it each time they work on a new design. The rapid development of technology in areas such as building materials has facilitated their own rapid evolution and they have made a point of making use of new materials or techniques as soon as they become available. The partners have worked extensively in the area of hospital design, and it can be said that the Kolan Hospital, Ankara Memorial Hospital, Ankara Liv Hospital, and Ulus Liv Hospital are based on the same design language. Even in these cases however, the hospitals have different details and characteristics that make each of them unique. The differences are such that it is only in making a close examination of the project that it becomes apparent that the same language is being used to put different concepts in place. For Zoom/TPU, the matter of design language is a fluid one, both in terms of the appearance of their work and in its evolution. Clearly the language has continued to develop over time, profiting from lessons learned with each project. A style runs through their work, which is the basis for their "language" but they continue to willfully change and develop the elements of that style.

Following the Lead of the Client

The focus of Zoom/TPU on hospital design has not only been a matter of their choice, but also of the direction of the Turkish economy. Where tourism may have thrived as a source of new architecture at a certain time, investors have clearly seen the advantages of creating modern hospitals at a high international standard in recent years. This is because large numbers of foreigners come to be treated in Turkey, as well, of course, as the more predictable Turkish base for the clientele. Some differences in their approach to hospital design find their origin in the attitude of the investors or health-care companies that control the institutions. It is clearly felt that good design is a positive element in health care, surely a relatively recent discovery in some circles. Some clients or investors place an emphasis on monumentality, which may well represent an indication of trustworthiness, while others believe that patients should feel as good as possible in a hospital environment. Zoom/ TPU's style has been varied to meet with these different demands.

Atilla Kuzu and Levent Cirpici both believe that the hospital environment should reflect the high-technology machines that are being used in the contemporary world of health care. The latest MRI scanners have a very contemporary design, for example, and that implies that the spaces around them should reflect this "high-tech" aesthetic. They have been criticized for creating environments that look too much like a "spaceship" but they firmly believe that the underlying aesthetic they employ is embedded in the very nature of the health-care sector. They do not see any difference between the form of an MRI scanner capsule and the components they use in their projects. Rather, robots that can carry out delicate operations symbolize the era that we live in, so too, they hope, do Zoom/TPU projects.

In a broader sense they feel that this type of design is in the spirit of the times. Many years ago medical devices were designed to look very solid with rough edges, but now they have many more organic curves—closer to the human body and spirit. Atilla Kuzu and Levent Cirpici say that the real reference for their designs can be found in the most modern medical devices, rather than in other, less sensitive environments. They believe that this design style

Quotes and statements attributed
to the partners of Zoom/TPU are
based on a written interview with
questions formulated by the author
and carried out in Istanbul by Funda
Mehter on 23 September 2014.

1 Evidence-based design (EBD)
is the process of basing decisions
about the built environment on
credible research to achieve the best
possible outcomes.
The Center for Health Design
created the evidence-based design
accreditation and certification
(EDAC) program to establish
a definition and process for
incorporating EBD into design.
Today, EDAC is an internationally
recognized program that awards
certification to individuals who
demonstrate an understanding of
the application of EBD in the design,
construction, renovation, expansion,
and replacement of health-care
facilities.
See www.healthdesign.org/edac
accessed on 30 September 2014.

2 See www.healthcaredesigmagazine.
com accessed on 30 September
2014.

3 See www.healthcaredesigmagazine.
com/article/five-need-know-
trends-shaping-healthcare-design
accessed on 30 September 2014.

has a healing effect on patients. "In a way," they state, "we have engaged ourselves in an effort to change the image of the hospital, trying not to make it look like a hospital but, instead, implementing 'good design'."

In the Maslak Acibadem Hospital (see page 85) they have used the stylized forms or image of a library in the entrance area, instead of a purely nursing environment, to encourage visitors and patients to be silent in the tranquil areas of the institution, propagating an indirect but effective "humanistic" message. They are seeking to create pleasing spaces that increase the awareness of visitors in all of their hospital projects. They believe in "Healing Environments" and in their physical and psychological effects. From entrance lobbies throughout the interiors of the spaces where they have worked, Zoom/TPU above all creates a feeling of continuity and thus of a steadiness of purpose. Given that patients place their health and thus their future in the hands of an institution, they rightfully expect a concentrated effort to cure them or to help them for whatever reasons they walk through a hospital door. That concentrated effort is embodied in the continuity of the designs of Zoom/TPU—a graduated process that starts with small details and ultimately creates a feeling of trust.

Evidence-Based Design

The success of Zoom/TPU in the hospital design field in Turkey has been such that they may well have done away with the very image of the "old-fashioned" hospital. This has resulted in an increasing number of proposals. The relationship between design and health care is an idea that has been extensively developed in Western countries. There are foundations and research centers dedicated to the areas that are called "Evidence-Based Design" or EBD[1] and "Health Care Design Ideas,"[2] which is the title of a magazine. These institutions have been the source of a number of ideas that Zoom/

Parametric design elements were used in the main entrance for the walls, ceiling, and tiling of Ulus Liv Hospital.

TPU has validated and employed in their own projects. *Healthcare Design* writes: "To support the connection between patients' comfort and their therapeutic advances, forward-looking health-care facilities are taking steps to imbue spaces with residential warmth. Borrowing from the 'home away from home' aesthetic that has served the hospitality industry well, these facilities are now reducing environmental stressors—moving away from traditional clinical designs in favor of what is more familiar to patients. The ultimate goal is to create interiors that make patients feel as comfortable as possible while still providing an efficient care model."[3] Investors and users in Turkey have also come to accept the reality of the relationship between design and health care, and they believe in it.

Looking at Koolhaas and Hadid

The partners of Zoom/TPU have an excellent knowledge of contemporary design and architecture. Amongst the figures they admire most, they cite Norman Foster, Richard Rogers, Philippe Starck, Rose Lovegrove, Jean Nouvel, Jean-Marie Massaud, Marc Newson, and Jasper Morrison. They have been inspired by the work of Tadao Ando, as well as by Zaha Hadid. They point out that Hadid's style has developed over time, but has always maintained its coherence. They have been following her since 1989, when she was closer to Deconstructivism, and they note an evolution in her work, but also its consistency with her early designs. From Rem Koolhaas/OMA they have found inspiration in a way of grouping functions and connecting them to users. In fact, these two references to the style of Hadid and the method of Koolhaas explain a good deal of the work of Zoom/TPU. Their flowing lines, or walls and ceilings that seem to have no distinct break, do on occasion bring to mind the interiors of Zaha Hadid in a way that does not go to extremes, but, rather, absorbs and identifies the needs of clients and users.

Fantastic Voyage

While maintaining their style, Zoom/TPU does, indeed, seek differing sources of inspiration according to the projects concerned. In this respect they cite the theme of the Maslak Acibadem Hospital (see page 85), which is based on human epithelia, while on the other hand Ulus Liv Hospital (see page 159) seeks ideas in its design from the immune system. "We come across so many germs and viruses during the day, our magical immune system protects us from those and removes them from our system," they say. "Basically, Ulus Liv Hospital symbolizes this reality by saying 'If you come in to the hospital, you will leave healthy'." By starting with details that might be described as "microscopic," the designers build on forms and concepts that form a logical, coherent whole. This might well bring to mind the 1966 science-fiction film in which a submarine is miniaturized to be able to navigate the interior of a human body. Like the 1864 Jules Verne novel *Voyage to the Center of the Earth, Fantastic Voyage* allowed for the creation of an entire universe of forms and colors that are known but are somehow not familiar. In the work of Zoom/TPU, in particular in the hospital context, the epithelium has an indisputable reality that they used as a source of inspiration. The immune system is the basis for life and thus is also a profoundly legitimate reference.

Material and Spatial Continuity

For the partners of Zoom/TPU, their most important project to date has been the Ulus Liv Hospital (see page 159), because it increased their self-confidence. The synergy and communication with the client in this instance was very successful, and they feel that they were supported and even embraced by the client on many levels. They are particularly proud of the visual details used in the project, and it is surely such careful detailing that has won them

Afrodit Exclusive is one of the best examples of Zoom/TPU's retail design approach.

accolades for their work. The complexity of the Ulus Liv project was such that some felt it could not be done, and yet Zoom/TPU succeeded beyond even their own expectations, creating a kind of higher level of self-awareness and capacity to take on new work. The design of the Ulus Liv Hospital emphasizes material and spatial continuity, a kind of integrated environment, where it seems apparent that each step a patient takes is leading to an efficient, modern treatment.

For the showroom projects such as Derimod, Continuum, Tiara Jewellery, and Afrodit, it is the objects to be displayed that serve as the reference points for Zoom/TPU's designs. Zoom/TPU, to the greatest extent possible, uses materials and supplies that are produced by or are related to the brand. For their fair stands they have mostly used the brand's own products, but applied them in a different perspective. This can be seen in the 2010 and 2011 Aspen stands (see pages 113 and 139). Zoom/TPU seeks to use the products involved, but not in the most visible manner. "What we want," they say, "is to use these products in a smart and aesthetic way; by creating a space with the products in order to emphasize them." In this manner, each project is based on a kind of "philosophic substructure." They do a great deal of research and the designs are based on their investigations. Whatever the subject, Zoom/TPU looks for what might be called the "cellular data" of each project as though they were taking the miniature submarine of *Fantastic Voyage* deep into their subjects. By learning at the closest level of the reality of the situations into which they are plunged, the designers then seek to synthesize their knowledge into forms, colors, and lighting that express what is happening inside. They get closely involved in the details and create themes that refer to the data that they uncover. Thus, for their hospital work, they refer to the human body, and to the immune system for example.

Furnishings and other surfaces are connected to wall or floor surfaces, making them appear not to be incidental additions to the hospital environment but essential parts of a logical and very contemporary process. As compared to the clutter of ugly leftover furniture and often worn-out materials and surfaces seen in many older hospitals, the design process carried out by Zoom/TPU makes it clear that here, patients will receive the best available care. The idea that space itself, lighting, floor, ceiling, and wall coverings play a role in medicine is now clearly established. A depressing, institutional environment that can be likened to an old railway station, or, worse, to a prison has a demonstrable, negative effect on patients, who must concentrate their own energy on curing themselves with the aid of a modern hospital. In this sense, Zoom/TPU is travelling not only into the proverbial body of the patient but also into his or her mind. Since the desires of investors or health-care firms are also integrated into their process, what Zoom/TPU is doing is more than pure, visually or aesthetically oriented design; it is about the underlying factors that motivate clients and thus the people they serve. Here, design becomes part of a cohesive process where each part plays a necessary role.

Flowing Like the Wind

The partners also refer quite willingly to their furniture design in evoking the projects that they feel are the most important for their career and the work of their office. The Taklamakan bench designed by Atilla Kuzu was chosen for the collection of MARTa Herford, a Frank Gehry-designed museum in Germany. This design has had a major impact on the Zoom/TPU office because it has been used in many projects over the years. The form of the bench was inspired by the Kazakh desert and movements along the Silk Road. Its curving lines are sliced into the wood as though its surface had been exposed to winds over time. For Atilla Kuzu: "The Taklamakan bench

Sound waves were the source
of inspiration for the woodwork
in the SALT Auditorium.

is like a part of the geography of Zoom/TPU." Despite the success of this bench, the partners shy away from using it too frequently in their interior design projects—they do not wish to be perceived as repeating themselves, but rather want to add to their "language" and to move forward. In fact, Atilla Kuzu has won numerous awards for his furniture designs. He was selected as "Designer of the Year" (Elle Decor International Design Awards, Turkey, 2010) while his furniture designs include the Best Design Award of Design Turkey Awards for his Angle table (2010); and his position as a finalist in the IFDA Wood Furniture Design Competition for Taklamakan (Japan, 1999). He was also selected as one of the thirty best designers from forty-six countries with his Barringer coffee table (International Furniture Design Fair, Asahikawa, Japan, 2002).

In their design for the SALT Galata Auditorium (page 121), Zoom/TPU proceeded with a method similar to that used for the Taklamakan bench, privileging only one material. Here, the design mentality and form of Taklamakan was carried over into an entire space. It was a great pleasure for Zoom/TPU to work on a project that was led by the respected Turkish architect Han Tumertekin. SALT is a non-profit cultural organization based in Istanbul founded in 2011. The director of research and programs at SALT is the well-known Turkish curator and writer Vasif Kortun. Many design and architecture groups were involved in the SALT Galata project, with each one asked to personalize the area for which they were to be responsible. Zoom/TPU imparted their own style on the auditorium, using their thoughts about the Taklamakan bench and using it to materialize sound waves in the auditorium. The relationship between the Taklamakan bench and the interior of the auditorium is immediately apparent to those who have seen both. In a way, sitting in the auditorium is a bit like being inside an enlarged version of the bench, with wood again playing a central role. Although the

designers themselves refer to "geography" when describing the Taklamakan bench, they could also have mentioned physiology, as in the voyage they take into the heart of their projects. Despite their concern with their own "language," the partners of Zoom/TPU are not so much creating a personal or firm style as they are seeking out the essence of what their clients or the users of their spaces want and need. It is this continuity that flows like a wind over their surfaces, smoothing angles, engendering a sense of unity.

The Figen and Servet Yazici Residence, which was shortlisted for the Aga Khan Architecture Award in 2001, was designed and built by Atilla Kuzu and Levent Cirpici when they were in their mid thirties. Here, they combined the qualities of youth with a great deal of care and application to the project that can only be equated with professional maturity. They see this as a project that was ahead of its time, especially where their treatment of differences in elevation and use of daylight are concerned. The goal was to interpret Mediterranean architecture in the specific context of Antalya, and in this they succeeded very well. The fact that the designers have demonstrated such a high level of accomplishment in an architectural project makes their interior work all the more substantive and significant.

Today, the goal of Atilla Kuzu and Levent Cirpici is to work more outside of their native Turkey, not so much for reasons of prestige as because of their admiration for European architects and designers. They have observed the architectural "culture" of Europe, with its high level of creativity but also its working style and even its regulatory environment, and they feel that they are well equipped to succeed there. In fact, their openness to work outside of Turkey is one of the main reasons for the publication of this volume. Zoom/TPU's experience in Turkey can certainly be applied in other countries, perhaps even reinforcing foreign

Above: The Taklamakan
bench designed by Atilla Kuzu.
Below: The interior of one of
Zoom/TPU's earlier projects, the
Figen and Servet Yazici Residence.

4 See www.cia.gov/library
   publications/the-world-factbook/
   geos/tu.html accessed on
   30 September 2014.

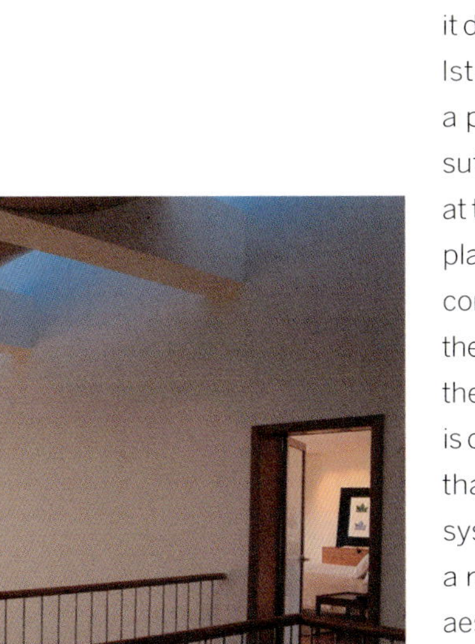

projects by bringing their familiarity with Turkish methods into a new set of circumstances. This desire to broaden their geographic base corresponds well to the designers' continual development of their architectural language as a function of new technological developments, and also to their presence in academic circles where new ideas emerge. Although Zoom/TPU has completed a large number of hospital projects, continuing in this area is not their priority. Rather, they feel that their methods and experience can be useful in such diverse areas as museums, archeological parks or urban planning projects.

Understanding the interest and importance of Zoom/TPU may also have something to do with situating Turkey in the world environment. Turkey has a population of eighty-one million people. The real growth rate of the economy (GDP) was 8.5% in 2011, although it dropped in the two subsequent years.[4] The country's largest city, Istanbul, one of the world's most significant historic capitals, has a population of more than 11.2 million people. These facts may suffice, together with the location of the country and Istanbul itself at the juncture between Asia and Europe, to explain why Turkey has played an increasing role in regional and world politics, and also why construction, architecture, and design have become strong points of the economy. The design approach of Zoom/TPU, which plunges into the details of every project, is certainly applicable in other contexts. It is one that privileges knowledge of the subject, and a design strategy that somehow incorporates the fundamentals, like the immune system in a hospital or sound waves in an auditorium. Coupled with a real taste for contemporary materials and technology, and an aesthetic penchant for flowing, dynamic surfaces, careful attention to lighting and furniture, and a kind of accumulation of details that make a coherent whole, Zoom/TPU is more than an interior design firm, it is one that crosses barriers and defines new territories.

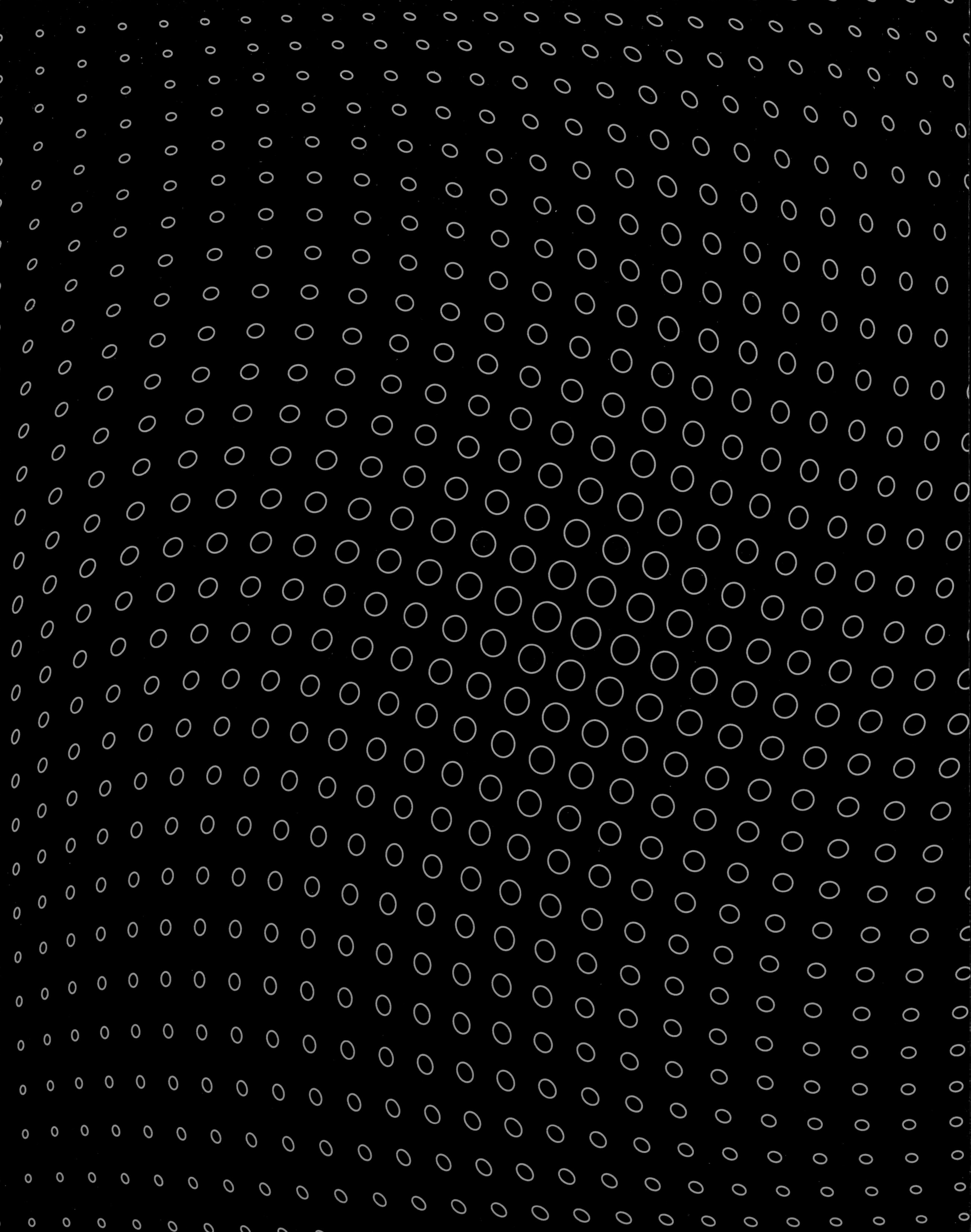

Blurring the Disciplinary Boundaries of Design: Zoom/TPU
by Celal Abdi Guzer

Zoom/TPU, which was founded by Levent Cirpici and Atilla Kuzu, represents a unique presence in Turkish design. The office works on different scales of design, ranging from furniture to interior design, right up to the scale of buildings and even urban planning. They sometimes act as contractors when they directly build or realize their own projects. The coexistence of these different types of activity within the same office may be seen as a sort of artisan's model, when compared with the contemporary tradition of architectural offices that are increasingly dependent on scale and subject-based specialties. Zoom/TPU's position defines contextual advantages and ensures the quality of production insofar as the Turkish design and construction market is concerned. On the one hand, the office gains a critical distance with its own production, where a project becomes subject to multiple types of feedback from different scales and alternative positions; on the other, a critical consciousness exists toward different stages of design and construction. Another advantage of such an organizational model is to avoid any style or typology-based reproduction. In this sense the accumulation of their work, developed over a period of twenty years, represents a scale, style, subject and typology-based plurality more than anything else.

In the Turkish design tradition, interior design had widely been recognized as having an independent scale and being a separate field of expertise. This scale-based separation was accepted as legitimate not only in the actual design market but also in architectural education. Such independence, on the one hand, encourages a reductionist approach, but, on the other, the end product runs the risk of an overt consistency of language. This risk is obviated in many projects realized by Zoom/TPU by the coexistence of different scales. Even for projects where they are not commissioned to work on all scales, it becomes possible to put in

place a critical understanding that blurs the scale-related differences. At the scale of building design, for example, the sensitivity toward construction elements or details can be based on an accumulation of knowledge fed by the interior or furniture scale. In a similar way, interior design always tends to become either an integral part of the architectural scale or expresses a consciously transformed identity with reference to the architecture.

In recent years Zoom/TPU has become one of the leading actors in hospital and health-care design in Turkey. When the program-based complexity and scale-based continuity of such a typology is considered, this is not accidental. In hospital buildings, the coordination of different scales and a multidisciplinary sustainability is inevitable. In this sense the design approach and accumulation of different scales practiced by Zoom/TPU create an alternative ground for resolving such complexities. On the other hand, hospitals are not only just technical buildings for Zoom/TPU; they are continuously improving their design strategies through research that tends toward generating an alternative cognition and experience of such environments. In their approach, hospitals are no longer mere nursing environments but rather a social space where visitors are to be distanced from their anxieties as much as possible.

The other characteristic of the design group is their sensitivity to details, which is also represented by the name of the company. Especially on an interior scale, instead of simply bringing together available products, they regularly develop new products or force market producers to make contextual, project-based alterations. In this respect it becomes possible to create unique interiors, lighting, materials and, finally, an alternative architectural language. For example the SALT Galata Auditorium is a unique example, where the bench developed by Atilla Kuzu is used to redefine a sitting arrangement and, with it, the whole interior environment.

Rendering of Ege Oncology Hospital.

This project demonstrates the language-based continuity between furniture and interior space developed by Zoom/TPU. In a similar way, a recent work, the Liv Hospital in Ulus, a ffirms a continuity between furniture, interior design and architecture, where interior scale transforms the architecture of an existing building to an alternative language.

Even in works realized by Zoom/TPU on the scale of the interior, one can easily follow the impact of the architectural scale where the design either becomes an integrated part of the building, or tends to transform the building itself. Their architectural work concepts use a more minimal language referring back to essential forms of architecture, contrary to the plurality of their inspiration as observed at the scale of the interior. Amongst these Ege Oncology Hospital, Parkim Chemistry Factory and Gebze Sheet Metal Factory can be mentioned as unrealized projects. Here a contextual significance exists, but there are conscious language differences between scales and projects. This context is not only defined by the physical setting of the projects but also by the establishment of representative limits of a cultural medium targeted within specific projects. Such contextuality allows the freedom to stay away from any pre-engagement with style or fashion-based continuity.

One of the rare examples of the single house scale in their work, the Figen and Servet Yazici Residence in Antalya that was shortlisted for the Aga Khan Architecture Award, defines language-based limits and the style-based freedom of the group. The regional and physical context of the building provides a background for minimalist language, where the complexity of details is reduced to merely a simplicity of form and the quality of light.

Istanbul, as a multilayered city of cultural pluralities, is an inspirational milieu for the group. The physical and cultural differences and richness of the city are reflected in Zoom/TPU's work in multiple ways. Within this plurality it becomes possible to develop continuous research, targeting different budgets and alternative cultural representations. Zoom/TPU not only develops simple projects modest enough to blend into everyday life, but also remains open to push the limits of design toward experimentation with new alternatives. Zoom/TPU's work represents a sense of continuity between international contemporary architecture and its adaptation to contextual and cultural circumstances. In this sense the developed projects must be seen as contextual modern alternatives to mainstream architecture. Especially for the typological development of the modern hospital, Zoom/TPU has contributed to international architecture by transforming the hospital from being a mere functional entity to an alternative living environment.

Within this singular existence, Zoom/TPU seeks an alternative model in terms of multidisciplinary office organization. In a way, it may be considered a compact model of integrated design where projects are not developed in a linear process but rather emerge through different scales and disciplines simultaneously. Within their work the artificiality of separating interior design from architecture becomes apparent. Blurring scales and disciplines not only improves the quality of work but also triggers research that leads to unique projects.

Celal Abdi Guzer is a Professor of Architecture at Middle East Technical University.

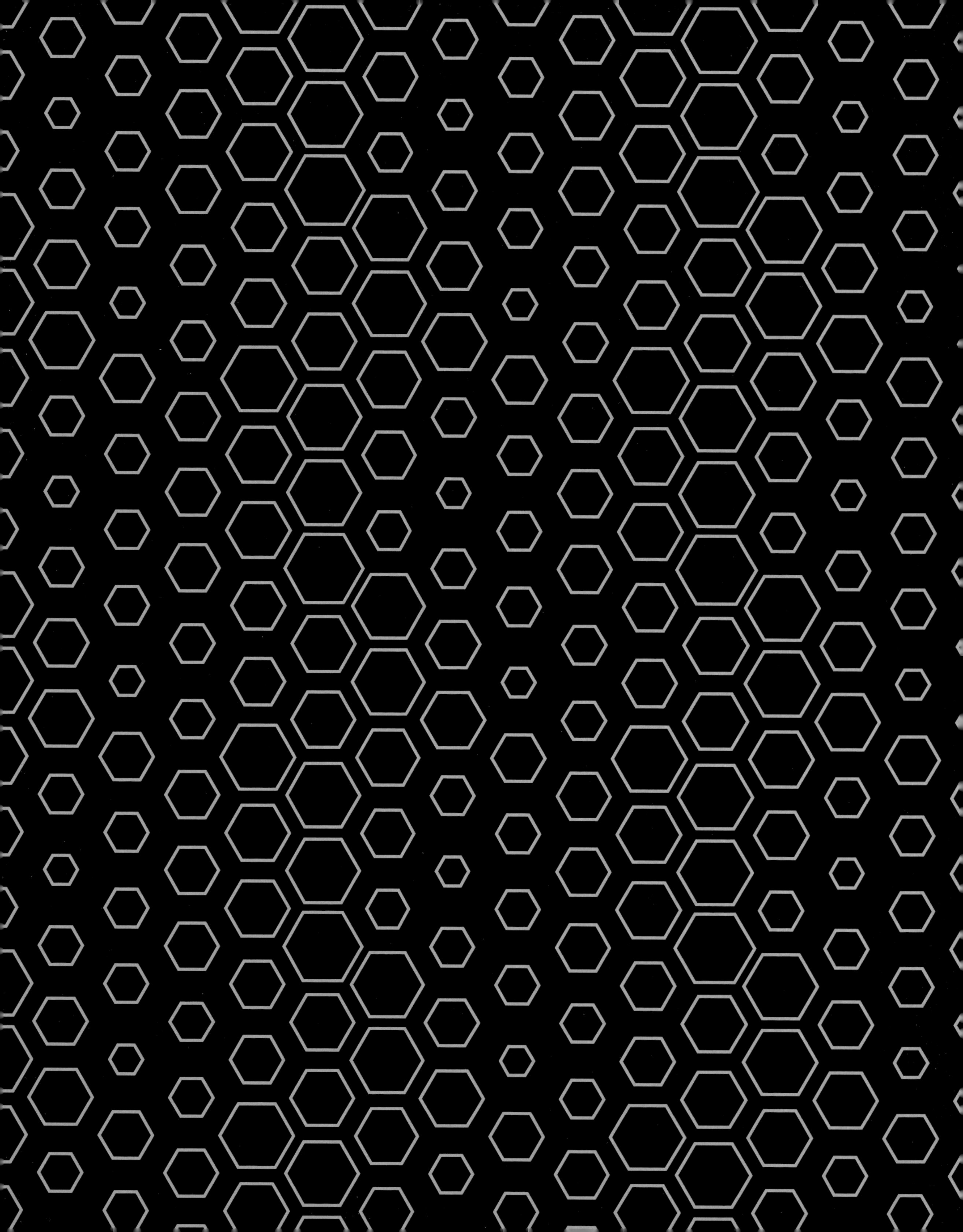

Featured Projects

ACIBADEM

Acibadem Clinic
Istanbul, Turkey, 2004
Area: 2800 m²

The Acibadem Bagdat Medical Center, which initially provided only outpatient services, was expanded and converted into a medical center in 2007 to meet increasing demand. It is located on Bagdat Avenue in a residential district located on the Anatolian or Asian side of Istanbul. The work of Zoom/TPU on the original outpatient polyclinic enterprise was intended to project an image of warmth, like that of a hotel, for patients entering the facility. Their brief provided that fifty-one percent of the space would be technical, and forty-nine percent would have a more aesthetic approach. The 2800-square-meter facility has eight floors, where air-conditioning, electrical systems, and even the reinforced-concrete construction and curtain walls were evaluated and reinterpreted according to the functions of the spaces concerned. Zoom/TPU worked with a number of difficulties for this project including floor heights insufficient for dropped ceilings, and three to four times more mechanical and electrical equipment than a normal building. Marble flooring, ceramics, laminate-coated MDF, gypsum-board ceilings, acrylic furniture, and carpeting were used by the designers for this project.

Main entrance.

ACIBADEM

ACIBADEM

Left page, top: Welcome counter
at the entrance.
Bottom: Patient examination
rooms near the waiting areas.

Below: Plan of the main entrance.

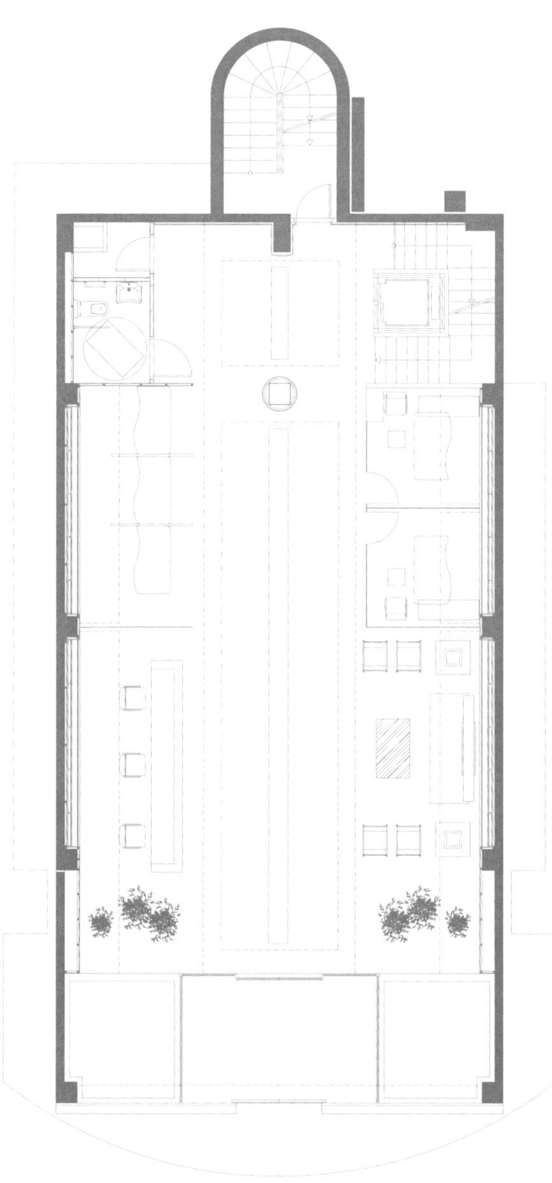

Below: The transparent
appearance of the hospital.

From lighting to seating, the main
entrance was specifically designed
by Zoom/TPU for this project.

Afrodit Exclusive
Istanbul, Turkey, 2006
Area: 120 m²

Located in the European part of Istanbul, Afrodit is a well-known clothing and accessories store that sells men's and women's apparel. The intention of the client and Zoom/TPU was to create a welcoming space in which customers are invited to freely touch and select products. The architects state: "We did not want to create an expensive image for the store that could have ruined the relationship with customers." Working with a space that was full of columns and a ceiling with numerous beams, Zoom/TPU decided to make organically formed holes in the ceiling plates in order to give an impression of height while not revealing the full, old ceiling. These forms create a "chain reaction" as they say. Ceiling lights designed by Herzog & de Meuron were chosen for this project by Zoom/TPU. The architects also played on the irregular positioning of some of the columns. They used elliptical, laser-cut, lacquered MDF panels for the ceiling and terrazzo for the flooring. The walls were "painted with a concrete texture."

Organically formed holes are the hallmark of the design for this store.

Left page, top: Customized irregular
ceiling details were used for the whole store.
Bottom: The plan of the ceiling pattern.

Below: The design of the showroom
emphasizes the harmony between the
lighting and the ceiling.

Pierre Cardin Osmanbey
Istanbul, Turkey, 2006
Area: 400 m²

Located in the Sisli district of Istanbul in the area of Osmanbey, this store for the noted French fashion brand Pierre Cardin takes into account the use of red and black in the corporate identity of the firm. The designers explain: "Forms referring to the logo of the firm that remains in the background were applied to the arrangement of the interior architecture. The store in Osmanbey has its distinct architecture with a historical aspect; therefore the structure of the interior space was designed in a way that this arrangement would not contradict with the existing building." The floors are in ceramic tile and mosaics, while the sales counters are in glass and stainless steel. Wooden shelves allow the merchandise to be well displayed, and wallpaper was employed for vertical surfaces.

The striking open area
created on the ground floor.

Left page, top: At the ground-floor level
a former floor was removed to create an
open area with an impressive spatial effect.
Bottom: Schematic plans of the ground
and first floors.

Below: A view of the subsequently
created mezzanine on the first floor.

ACIBADEM

Bursa Acibadem Hospital
Bursa, Turkey, 2006
Area 28,500m²

This hospital was purchased by the Acibadem Healthcare Group when its basic construction was partially completed. It is located in the district of Nilufer, a developing area of Bursa, which is a large city in northwestern Anatolia. The hospital was then restructured and opened as a health center working to the high standards of Acibadem. As was the case in the later Bakirkoy Hospital, the main materials employed by Zoom/TPU were marble, ceramics, laminate-coated MDF, gypsum-board ceilings, and acrylic furniture. Their intervention is immediately evident in the main entrance of the hospital, a spirit that also appears in the polyclinic waiting rooms, patient examination rooms, and corridors. Carpeting was chosen for the patient corridors that was intended to give patients a peaceful experience, unlike the usual hospital atmosphere. The waiting rooms receive direct sunlight and have frequent views of the landscape. In the materials and colors selected, as well as the finishing of the details, the Bursa Acibadem Hospital has sought to distance itself from the cold, literally "clinical" feeling of many health-care facilities. Zoom/TPU paid careful attention to details, giving the more public areas of the hospital a very different feeling than that which might be expected in such an institution.

Entrance lobby.

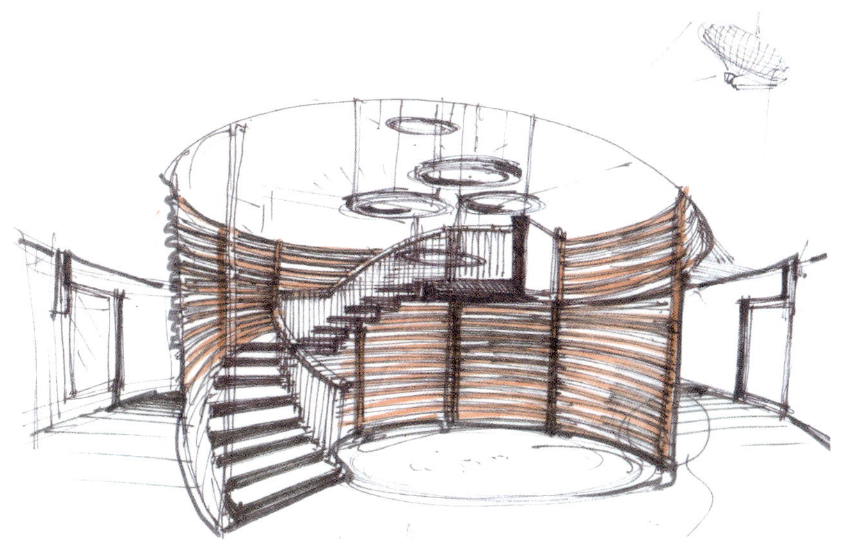

Left page: A detail of the stairs.

Above: Sketch of the staircase
and gallery area.
Below: Section of the stairs.

Following pages: The area of the
staircase was designed to capture
daylight and to spread it naturally.

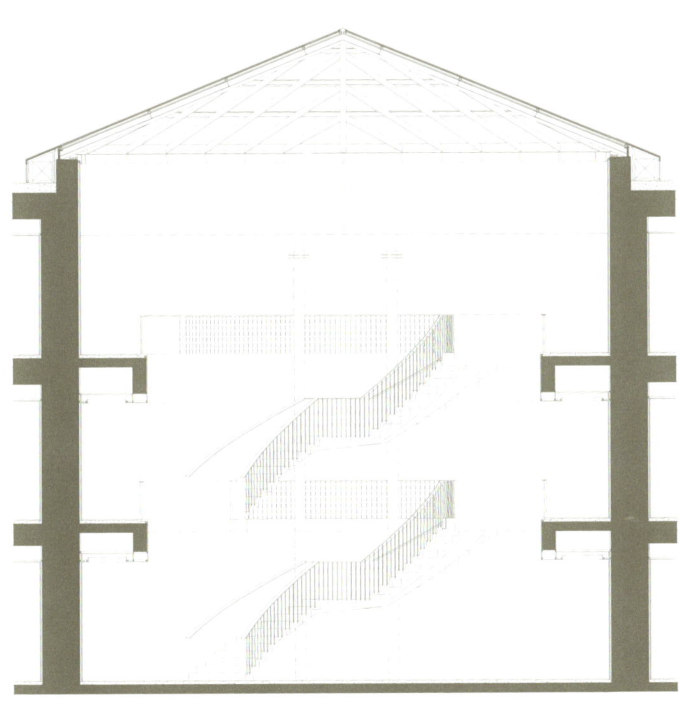

Below: Sketch of a bed head and gas
inlet details.

Right page: The bed unit, inlet, ceiling,
and lighting have been designed as a
coherent whole.

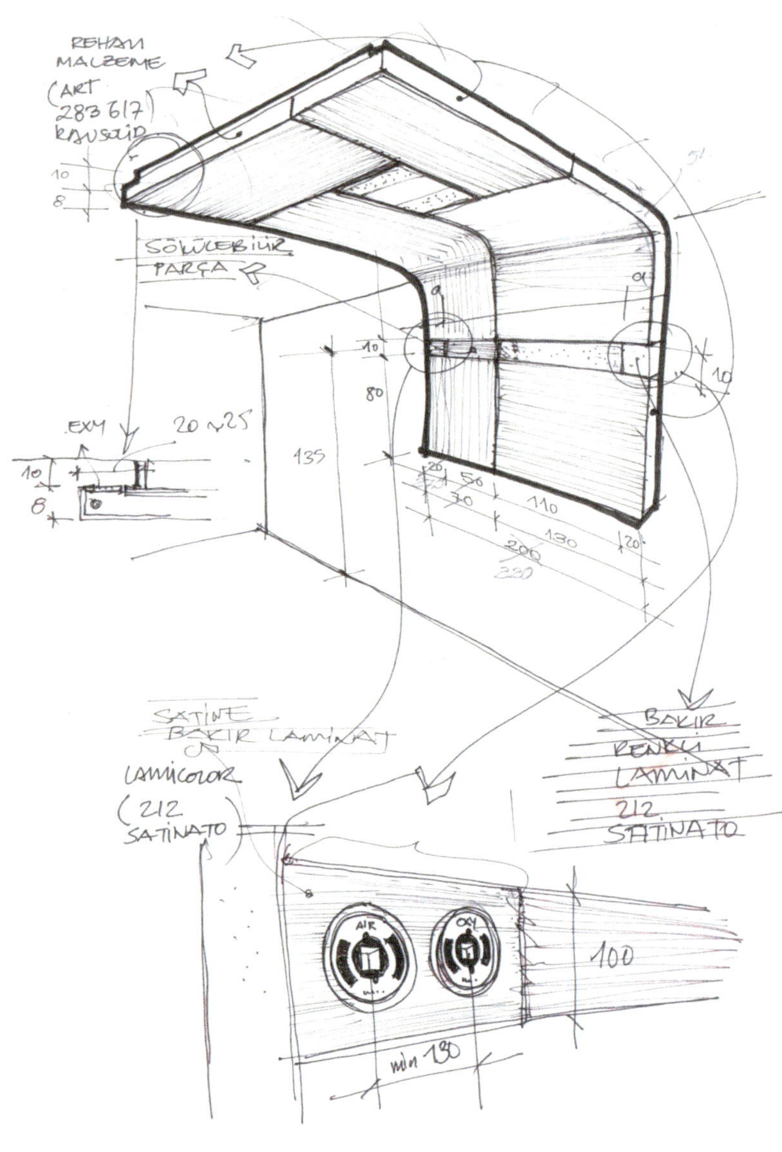

DERİMOD

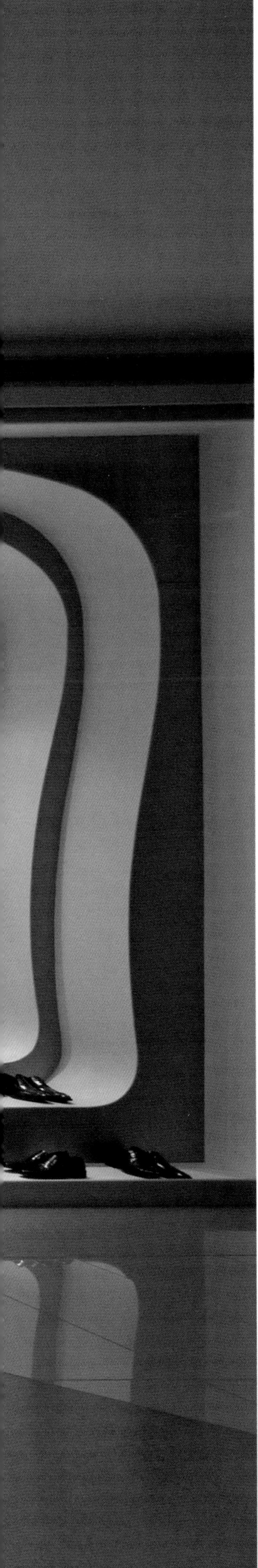

Derimod Capacity
Istanbul, Turkey, 2007
Area: 240 m^2

Derimod is a leather-goods outlet located in the Capacity Shopping Mall in the largely residential Bakirkoy area of Istanbul. Capacity, which opened at the end of 2007, has 130 shops and is the largest facility of its kind in this part of Istanbul. Zoom/TPU made use of organic forms on the exterior façade of the shop and on the window display shelves as well. Lacquered MDF was used as a wall covering, together with painted glass. Gypsum board and backlit vinyl are used for the ceiling. Units in the store are made of lacquered MDF. The focus is on bronze glass, wood, and shades of white. The shelving inside the store is, of course, in continuity with the organic appearance and organization of the shop façade.

Left page: The design of the exterior was conceived to highlight the layered arrangement of the interior and the window.

Below: Sketch of the exterior.

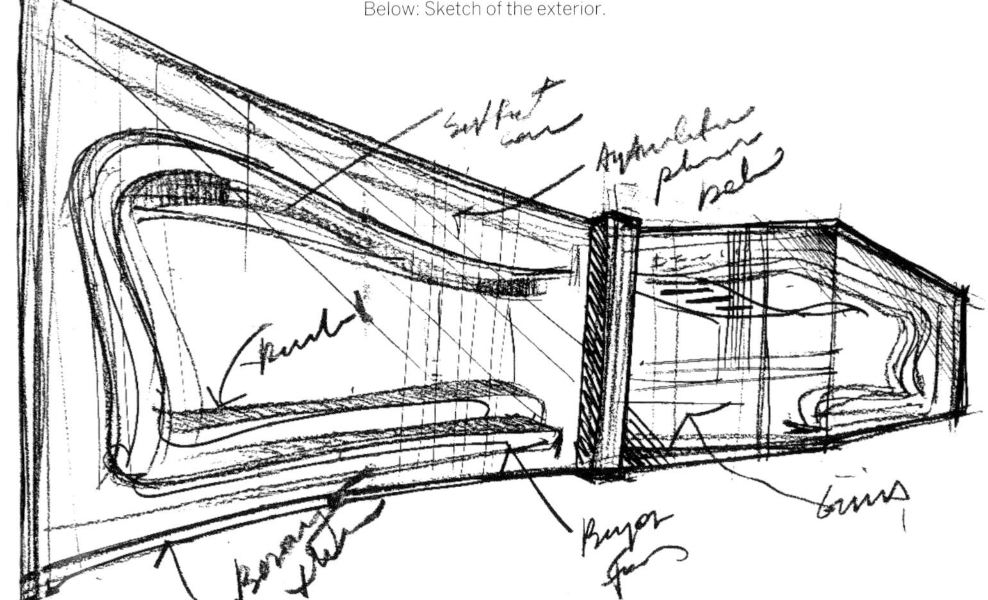

Below: Sketch of the interior.

Right page: Showcase elements
reflect the window design.

Yesilkoy Acibadem International Hospital
Istanbul, Turkey, 2007
Area: 20,000 m²

The Acibadem International Hospital is located in Yesilkoy, Istanbul, a residential district in the European part of the largest Turkish city. After taking over the institution, which had opened in 1989 as Turkey's first private hospital in the Western sense, the Acibadem Healthcare Group began a two-year renovation program to bring the hospital up to their standards in terms of technology, but also where the design is concerned. The goal, here as elsewhere in the hospital group, was to increase the comfort of both patients and staff. In parallel with the basic hospital services, private intensive-care rooms were upgraded for ethical and scientific reasons, as well as to ensure patient privacy. The hospital has kidney dialysis units, emergency observation beds, and post-coronary angiography observation units. Advanced imaging is performed with the 1.5 Tesla MR Magnetic Resonance Imaging Scanner, offering comfort to patients in the diagnosis and treatment of cancer. This medical effort was accompanied by Zoom/TPU with their usual attention to details, which involved not only a decorative aspect but real improvements in the comfort of users, both in a visual sense and in terms of the feelings generated by well-designed hospital spaces.

The dentistry clinic, a glass separator with indented glass work.

Main entrance waiting lounge, where
natural light has been used extensively.

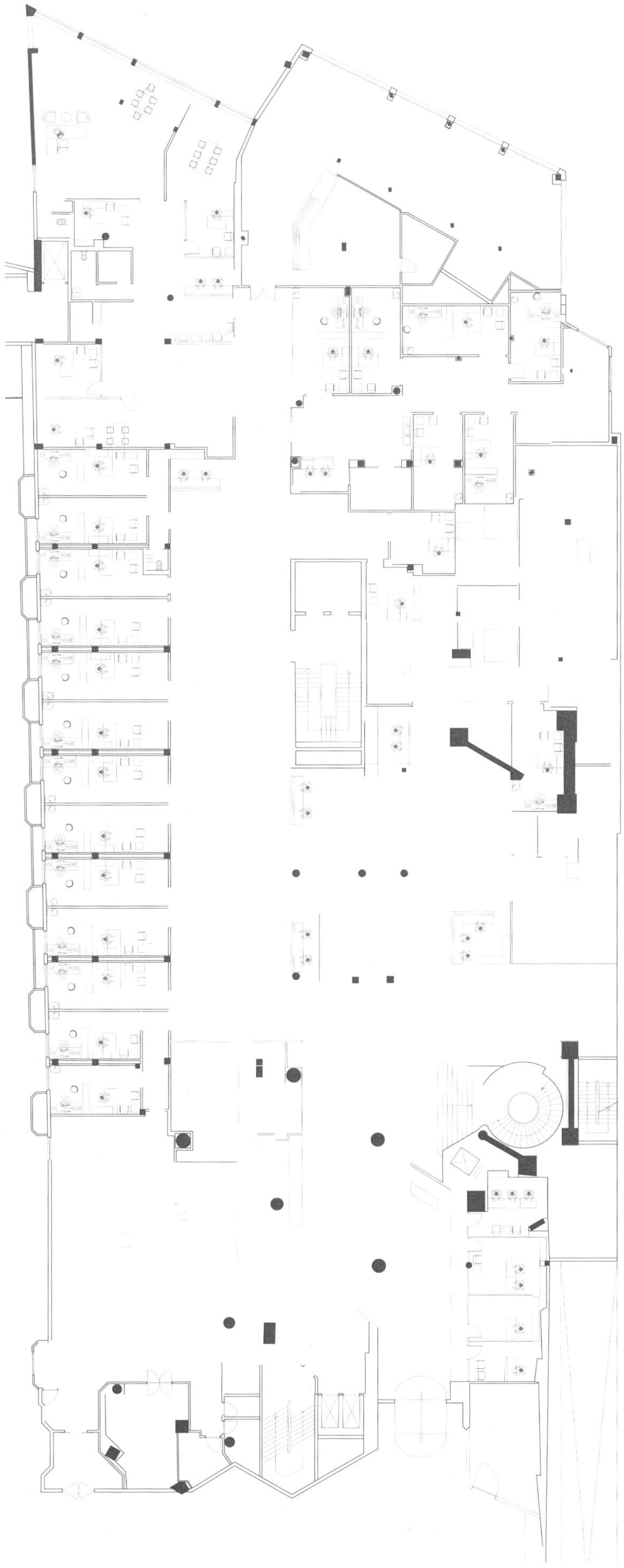

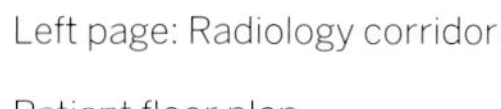

Left page: Radiology corridor.

Patient floor plan.

General views of the patient rooms.

Farmatek
Istanbul, Turkey, 2008
Area: 2200 m²

Farmatek is a Turkish firm active in the vitamins market, founded in 1996. These offices are located in Umraniye on the Asian side of Istanbul. The structure was built in accordance with the drug manufacturer and distributor's function and design to reflect a new institutional theme throughout. Steel construction was used for the façade of the gallery and white construction is maintained through the gallery with a similar lighting as the igniter of the transparent concept of the façade. All the units were composed with transparent sections as an extension of the transparency concept of the façade. The formerly cold atmosphere was improved with natural wood patterns, laminated MDF for the walls, and marble flooring. The seating units were made with fiberglass. Zoom/TPU chose lighting designed by Ross Lovegrove for this project.

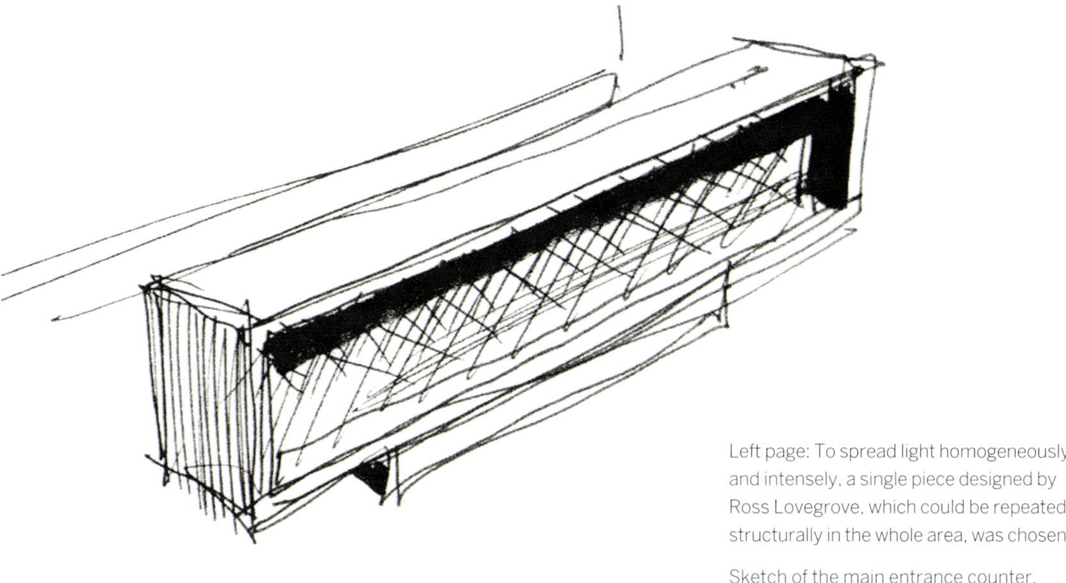

Left page: To spread light homogeneously and intensely, a single piece designed by Ross Lovegrove, which could be repeated structurally in the whole area, was chosen.

Sketch of the main entrance counter.

Below: Main entrance and gallery space.

Right page: Views of the offices and the
washroom area.

Dumankaya Modern Vadi Showroom
Istanbul, Turkey, 2008
Area: 1200 m^2

The Modern Vadi is a Dumankaya project located in Esenyurt on the European side of Istanbul. It includes eleven high- and medium-rise residential structures with a total of 1589 apartments, together with retail space designed by the Istanbul firm DBArchitects. Zoom/TPU designed the sales offices with natural stone on the floors; MDF is used for the sales units, which include screens for presenting the project, while an acrylic composite is used for the bar and the information counter. The double-height space is open and welcoming with a vertical wooden slat exterior.

Left and following pages: To allow various arrangements, Aziz Sariyer's seating group design called "Istanbul" has been used for the entire sales office.

LONDON
PARIS
İSTANBUL
TOKYO
NEWYORK
DANIŞMA
Information

Bakirkoy Acibadem Hospital
Istanbul, Turkey, 2008
Area 17,500 m²

In this interior renovation project, the main circular element of the original plan was retained, and the circular theme was expanded using organic forms for the detailing and other spaces, finally becoming the main design element of the entrance hall. The designers make frequent use of a two-tone scheme for the woodwork. Light and dark finishes are employed to underline differences in functions within the hospital. The use of "exaggerated" patterns in wallpapers and ceilings is meant to alleviate the dullness of repetitive units usually seen in hospitals. For the wood, as well as stones selected, Zoom / TPU gave a clear preference to "natural" finishes. Within the purely medical spaces, industrial products and finishes are the rule for technical reasons. The lighting scheme is considered a salient factor of the overall design with the goal of obtaining an indirect and calming effect. The main materials used for the project are marble, ceramics, laminate-coated MDF (Medium Density Fiberboard), gypsum-board ceilings, and acrylic furniture.

Ground floor main entrance.

Left: This was the first time that Zoom/TPU used such a circular arrangement for the patient corridors.

Above: A core was developed to
create a kernel with the elevator lobby
and the building's main structure.
Right: Nurse counter.

Roche
Istanbul, Turkey, 2009
Area: 6000 m^2

Located in the Sisli district of Istanbul, the Hoffmann-Roche pharmaceutical firm offices were designed with entrance walls in glass, laminate desks, closets with laminated patterned wood, glass partitions, and randomly placed hanging linear lighting elements. The arrangement of the light fixtures is intended to emphasize the "multidirectional" efforts of the firm, and indeed of the interior design itself. The logo of the firm, a lozenge shape, has been evoked on mirrored surfaces, door handles, and the ceiling lights. Conference areas and workstations were "designed as characteristic components of the project."

Façade detail of the conference room.

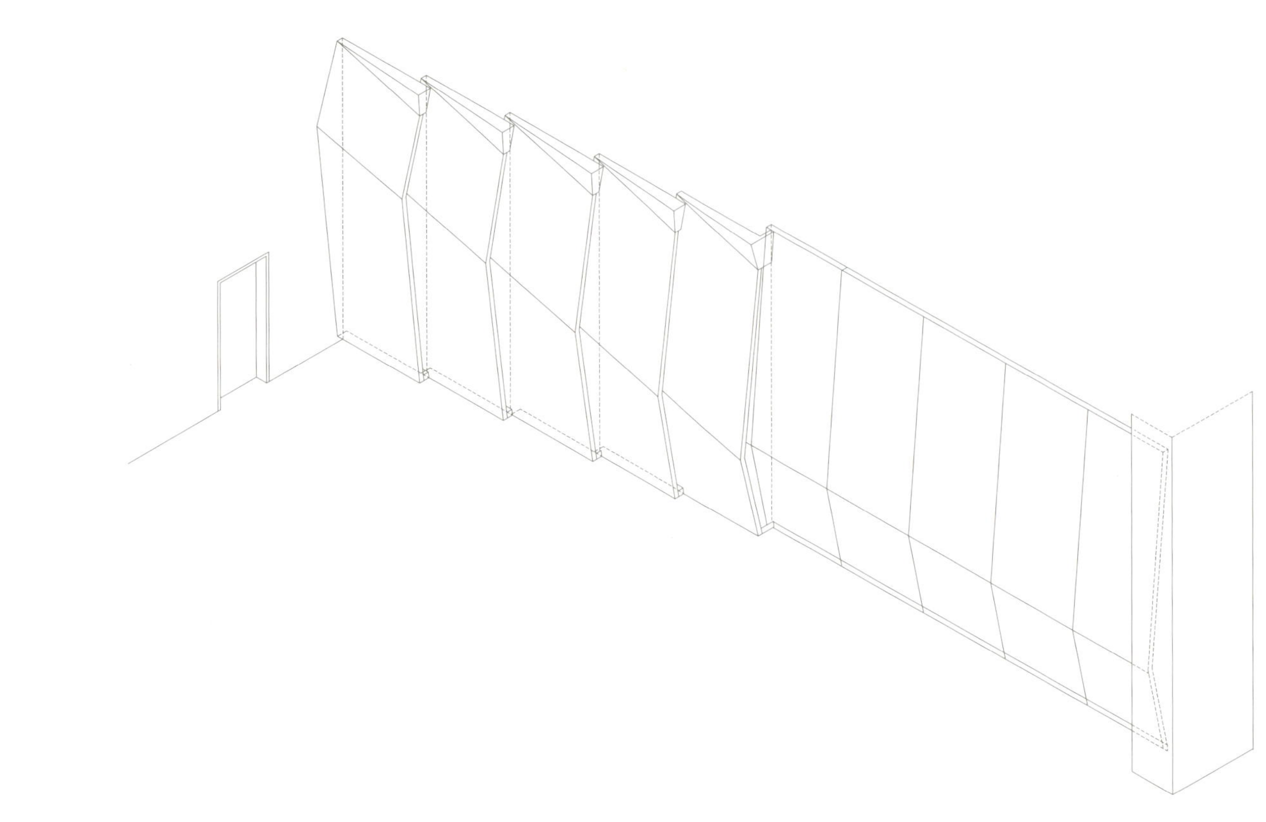

Left page, top: Isometric perspective
of the façade of the conference room.
Bottom: Foyer area.

Above: Wood surfaces were designed
for sound insulation on the inside of
the conference room.

Above: Office floor with view of
the personnel rest area on the right.

Right page, top: VIP day room floor sketch.
Bottom: The floor where VIP meeting
rooms are located.

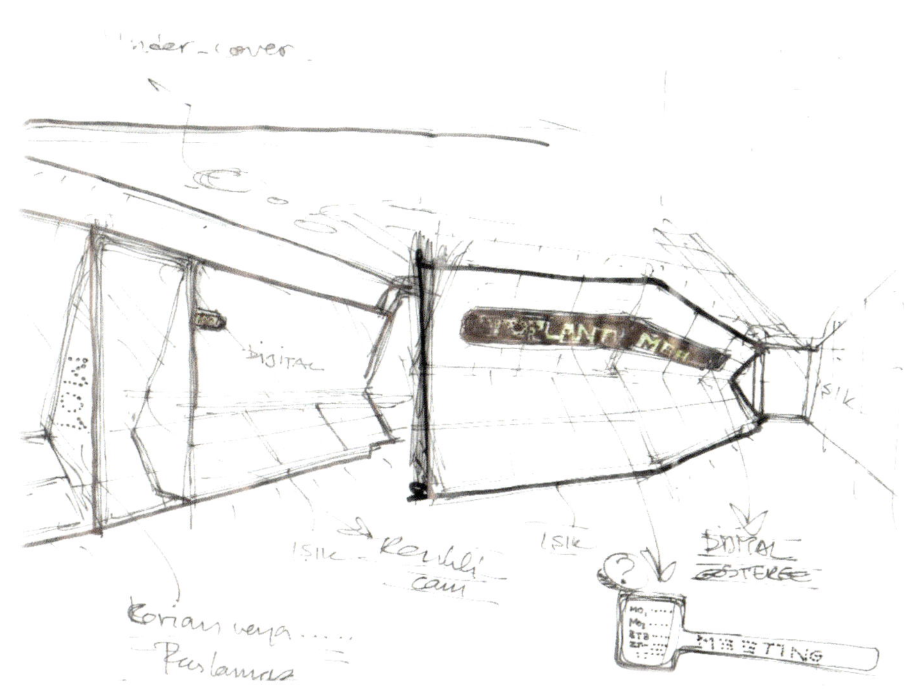

under-cover
DIJITAL
TOPLAND MAH
ISIK
ISIK
Renkli cam
ISIK
DIJITAL GÖSTERGE
Korian veya ...... Paslanmaz
MEETING

Teknik Oda

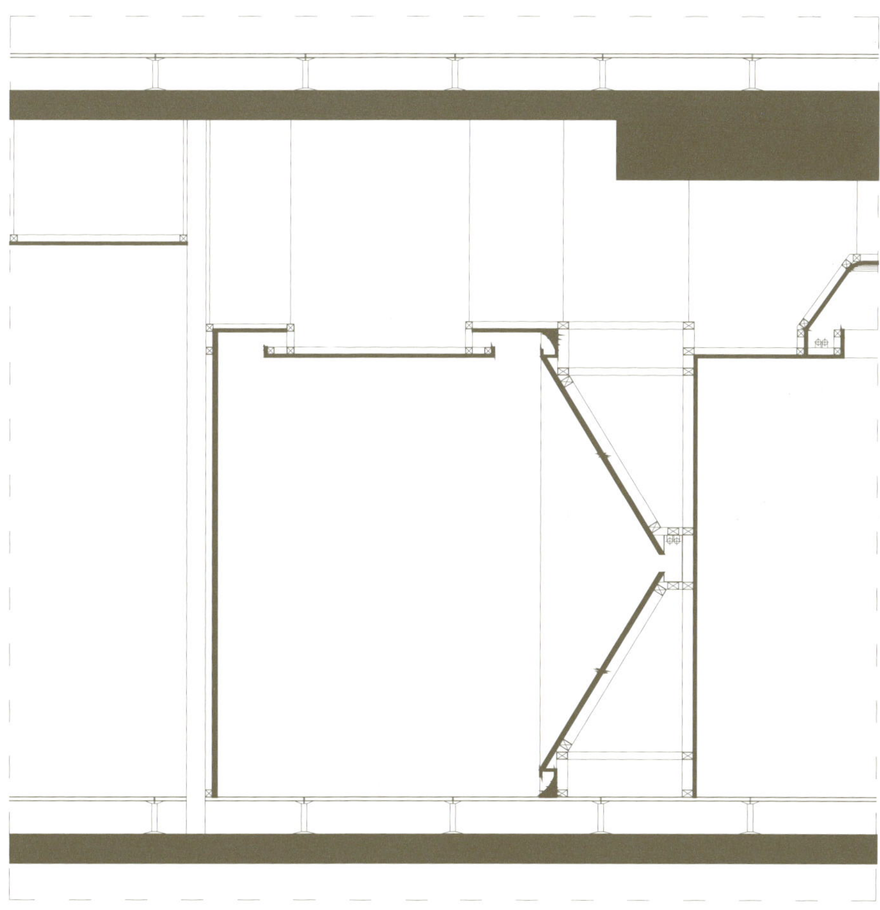

Left page: With a curvilinear wall on one side and a mirror on the other, the corporate logo of the brand was used indirectly in the office corridors.

Below: Section of the entrance of the office corridors.

Dumankaya Ikon Sales Office
Istanbul, Turkey, 2009
Area: 400 m^2

This is a sales office for the Dumankaya Ikon, one of the tallest residential projects in Istanbul—a three-tower, 149-meter-high complex. The plan of the three elliptical blocks in the forty-eight-story project served as a source of inspiration for the working units in the sales office and the bistro tables, where customers are welcomed and the project is explained. It is located in Kadikoy on the Asian side of Istanbul. Materials employed include composite plexiglas wall covering, acrylic composite used for the information counters, and LED lighting. Plexiglas composite and LED lighting are used for the column coverings, and acrylic carpeting was selected for the floors. Zoom relied in this instance on new materials to emphasize the contemporary aspects of the Ikon towers.

Left and following pages: The space arrangement was created to highlight the project's characteristic geometric elements.

NEW YORK
PARIS
ISTANBUL
DUBAI
TOKYO
YANGIN
FIRE HOSE

Maslak Acibadem Hospital
Istanbul, Turkey, 2009
Area: 40,000 m²

Maslak is a business area in Sariyer, the northernmost district of Istanbul. This hospital is voluntarily associated with a future trade center, and an area where several cultural and social facilities are located. Transportation is readily available and a subway stop connects directly to the hospital. Here the architects sought inspiration from a microscopic view of epithelial tissue, a kind of "crystalized net" that is used as the basic concept of the interior design. This stylized inspiration, materialized here in the form of a single plane, appears in floors and concealed ceiling light fixtures. Patients accede to their rooms in passages lit with this very specific technique. In the patient rooms, a continuous arc-shaped unit was designed to cover technical equipment and lighting components. This unit is intended to "give the patient the feeling that he or she is at the focal point of all attention and services." Carpet in patient areas, as well as acoustic ceilings and a double-glazed façade shell meant to keep out traffic noise, are also part of the strategy used by Zoom/TPU to increase the comfort of patients and visitors. The main materials employed here are marble, ceramics, laminate-coated MDF, gypsum-board ceilings, acrylic furniture, and the decorative composite panels referred to.

The view of the wall where
the information desk is located.

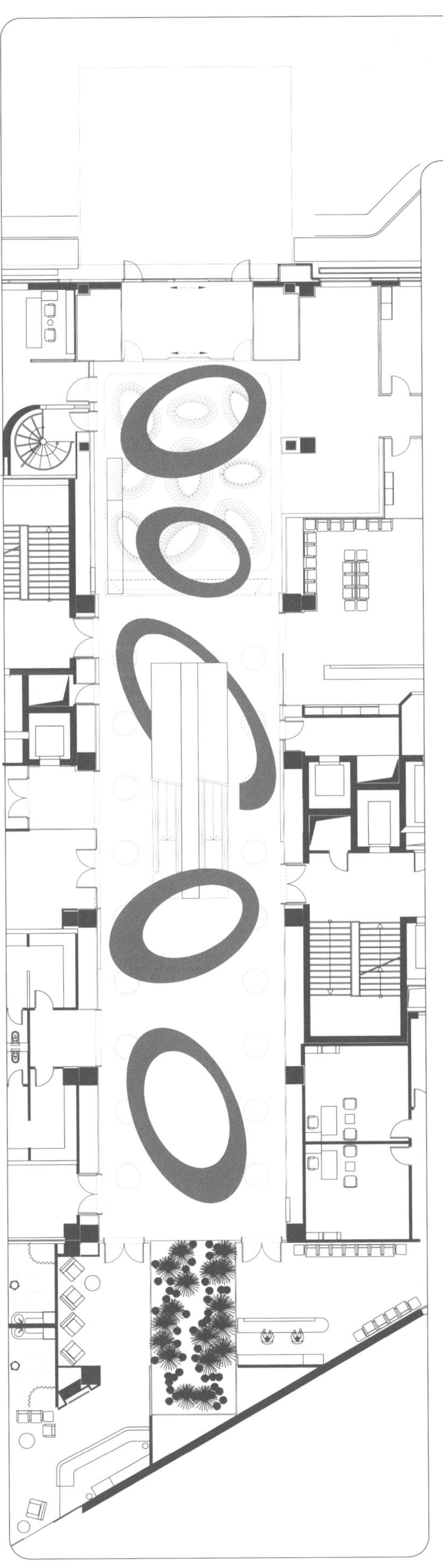

Left page: The façade of the transit
area that connects the two blocks.

Plan of the entrance lobby.

Following pages: Waiting area.

Looking along the hallway of the
dentistry polyclinic area.

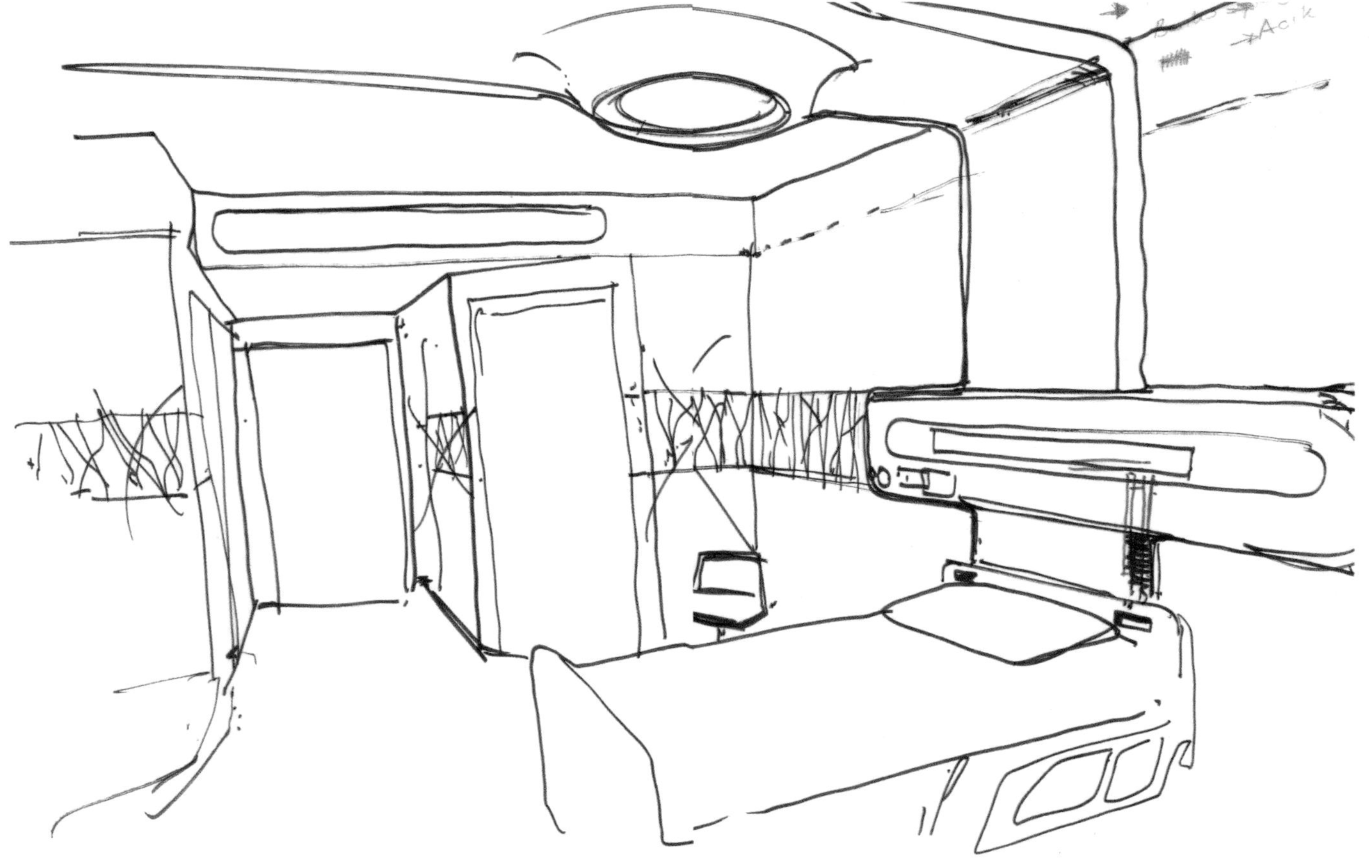
Açik

Conference room.

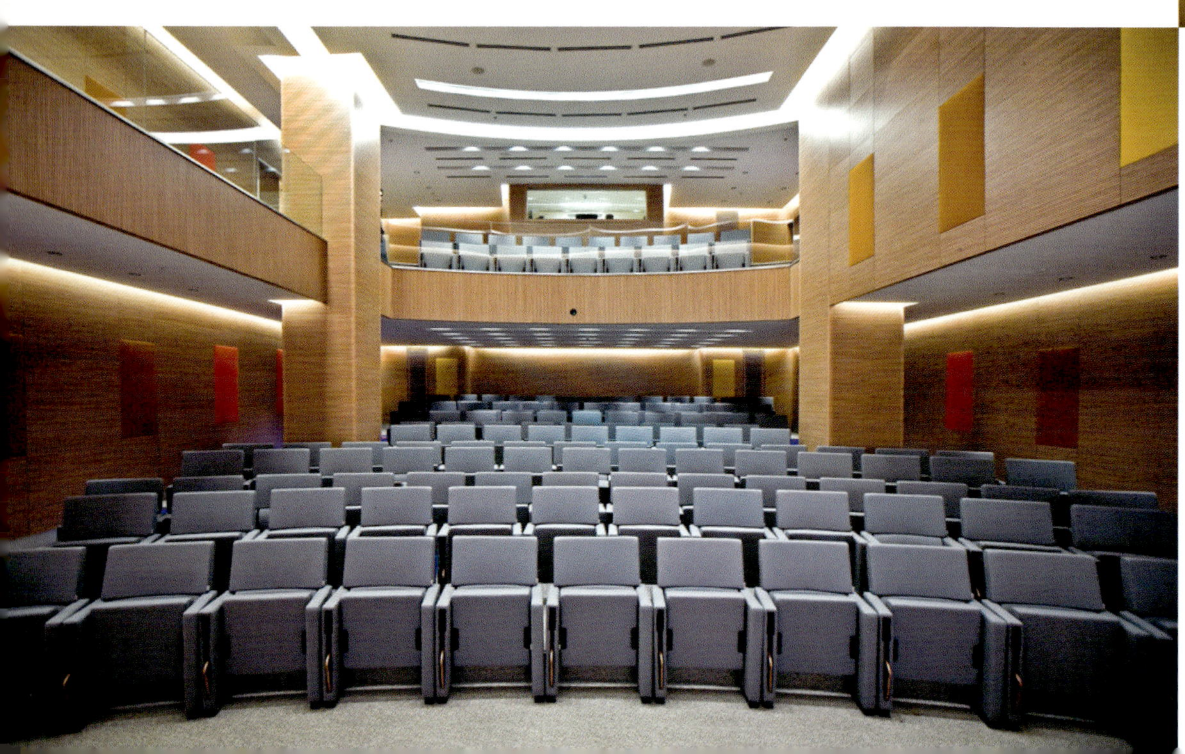

View of the cafeteria.

Tiara Jewellery
Istanbul, Turkey, 2010
Area: 300 m^2

Located in the old Sultanahmet area of Istanbul not far from the Blue Mosque (or Sultan Ahmed Mosque) the Tiara Jewellery store is in the Nakkas building, built over a 1400-year-old cistern that was protected with a metal frame. Porcelain is used on the floors and the walls are in natural stone. The dome-shaped ceilings are in gypsum board and black-painted aluminum. Sales counters are in glass and wood, and the lighting fixtures are custom-made. For the display cases and wall partitions, stylized Ottoman patterns are used to emphasize the historic nature of the district and the quality of the objects being sold. The designers explain: "It was aimed to adapt this design to the frequent presence of tourists and the limitation of time, while prioritizing the products."

Left page: At ceiling level, the original structure of the vault is used as an indirect light source to reflect light.

Sketch of the display unit.

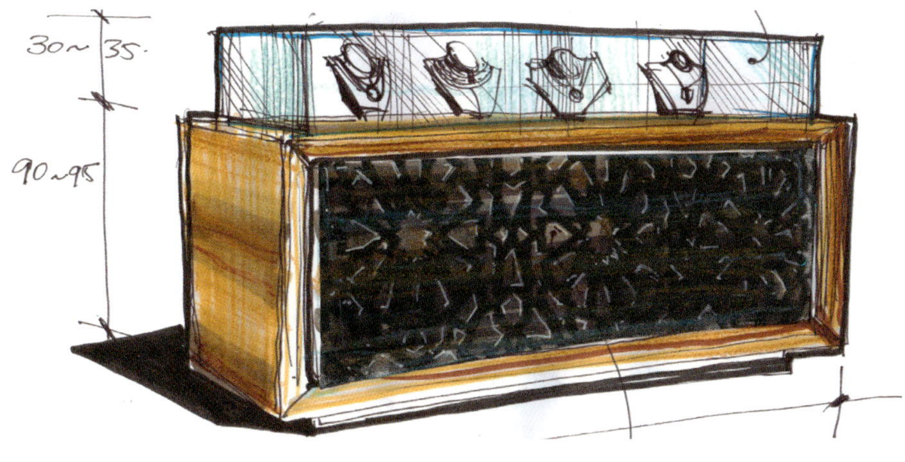

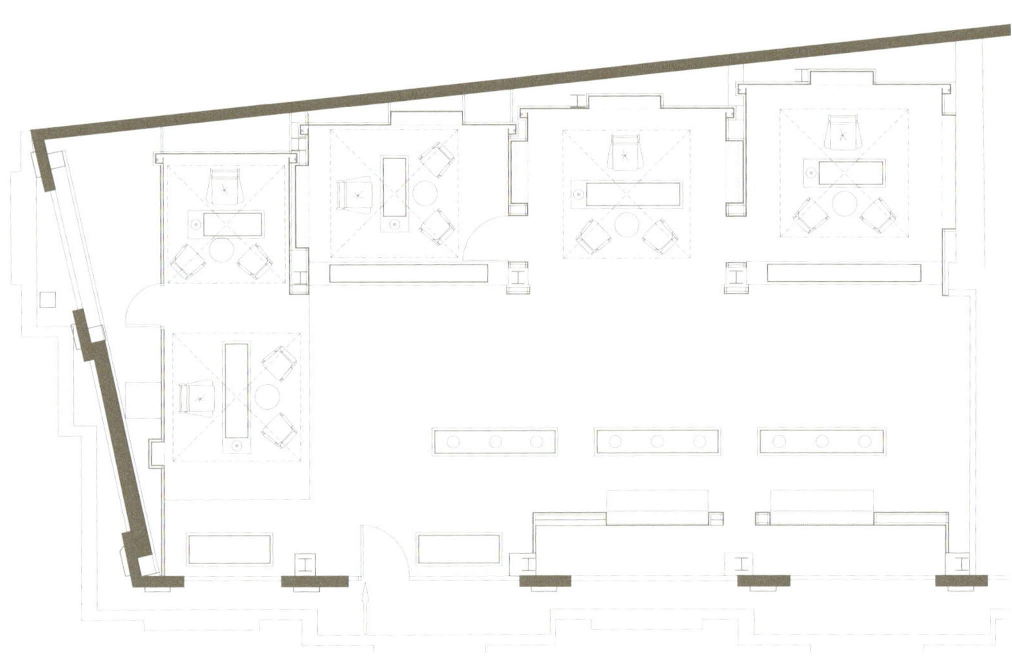

Left page, top, and here below:
Two general views of the showroom.
Bottom: Interior plan.

Right: A sketch of the interior.

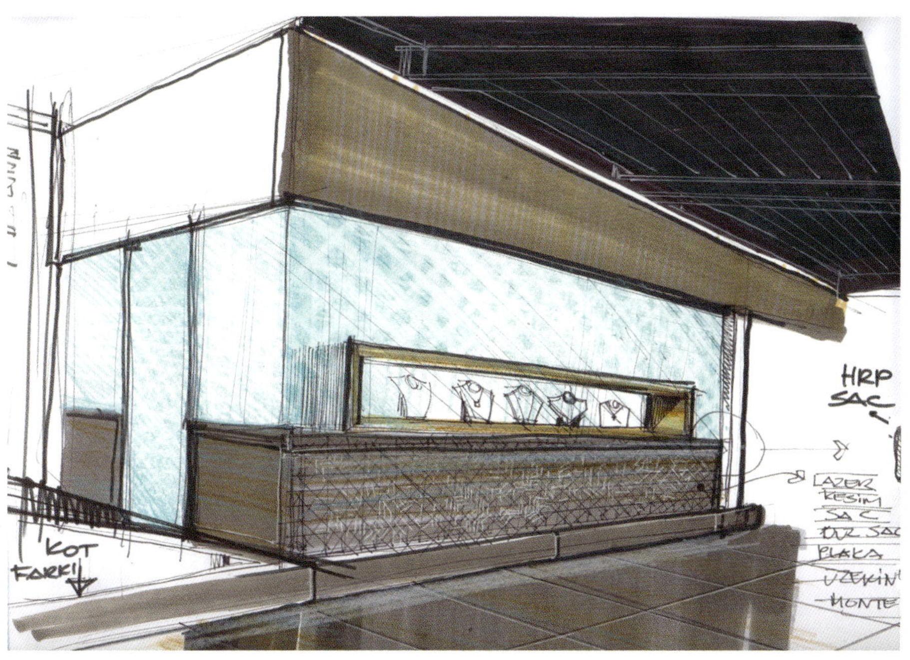
HRP
SAC
LAZER
RESIM
SAC
TOZ SAC
PLAKA
UZERIN
MONTE
KOT
FARKLI

MEMORIAL
2614

Atasehir Memorial Hospital
Istanbul, Turkey, 2010
Area: 5000 m^2

This modern facility is part of the effort of the Memorial Healthcare Group to "become a global brand by following scientific and technological developments, focusing on patient satisfaction, personnel, and making a difference in quality service with our advanced technology." Atasehir Memorial Hospital has a 143-bed capacity, modern architecture, comfortable patient rooms, and outpatient clinics that are "designed to positively affect patient psychology." This is very much part of the concept of Zoom/TPU for this facility located in the Atasehir area in the Asian part of Istanbul. Marble and antibacterial carpet, gypsum-board and illuminated vinyl ceilings, acrylic counters, and pendant profile lighting are amongst the materials used. The designers state that this project was "designed with homogenous lighting with more modern and transparent units in order to create a more spacious feeling than the group's Okmeydani Hospital. The Atasehir Memorial Hospital was detailed to create a modern but warm atmosphere."

Nurse station.

Left page, top: Patient corridor.
Bottom: Nurse counter.

Above: Main entrance counter.

Following pages: Waiting area,
lobby lounge.

INTEMA
MUTFAK
INTEMA
MUTFAK

Intema Showroom Nisantasi
Istanbul, Turkey, 2010
Area: 213 m^2

Intema is part of the large Eczacibasi industrial group. Eczacibasi's core sectors are building products, health care, and consumer products. The Intema store in the Nisantasi area of Istanbul offers "a complete solution in bath and kitchen products." According to the designers: "The main approach for this extension of the design products of the Intema group was to apply colors, backgrounds, materials, and lighting units in a harmonious way in order to exhibit the themes clearly and prevent distraction." Floors are in ceramic, while lacquered MDF is used for desks, and linear LED bands are inserted into the floors. Gypsum board with aluminum profiles covers the ceilings. Atilla Kuzu's "Open" kitchen design, winner of the 2010 Best Kitchen Design (Elle Decor International Design Awards, Turkey), is visible in the images for this project.

A linear light band is used to guide
the customer to the kitchen displays.

İNTEMA
MUTFAK

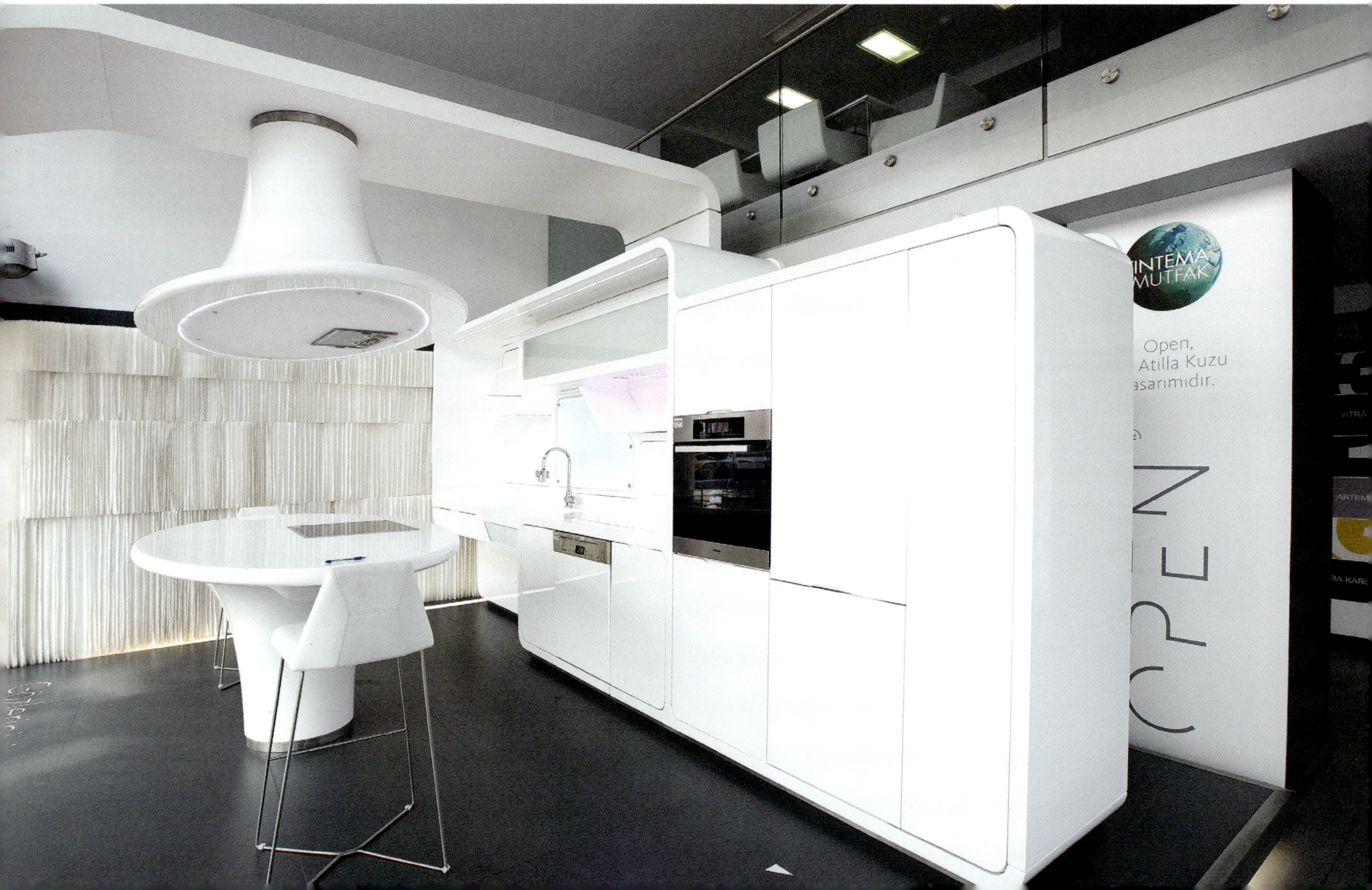

İNTEMA
MUTFAK
Open,
Atilla Kuzu
asarımıdır.
OPEN
VITRA
ARTEM

Left page, top: Sales area.

Two views of the "Open" kitchen designed by Atilla Kuzu and, right, a sketch of the "Open" kitchen for the Intema Showroom.

Medistate
LONDRA
PARİS
İSTANBUL
MOSKOVA
TOKYO
DANIŞMA
Information

Kavacik Medistate Hospital
Istanbul, Turkey, 2010
Area: 15,000 m² (total for hospital)

This very modern 120-bed hospital is located in the Kavacik area in the Asian part of Istanbul. The institution aims to provide "world-class health-care services at affordable prices." This is the first "environmentally friendly" hospital in Turkey. All materials used in the hospital are degradable or recyclable. Originally designed as an office building, the structure was converted into a hospital by different groups of architects. Thus the outpatient floors and other areas have different concepts. Zoom/TPU worked on areas such as the entrance level, stairs, information desk, and elevator area that were carefully designed to create an agreeable atmosphere for patients and their visitors. Dividers were specially designed to create privacy in the VIP area and transparent surfaces were covered in films with a vectorial pattern. In the VIP area, mirrors are used to make the space seem larger. As always, despite the rather heterogeneous architecture of this hospital, Zoom/TPU has succeeded in creating design continuity and a contemporary feeling.

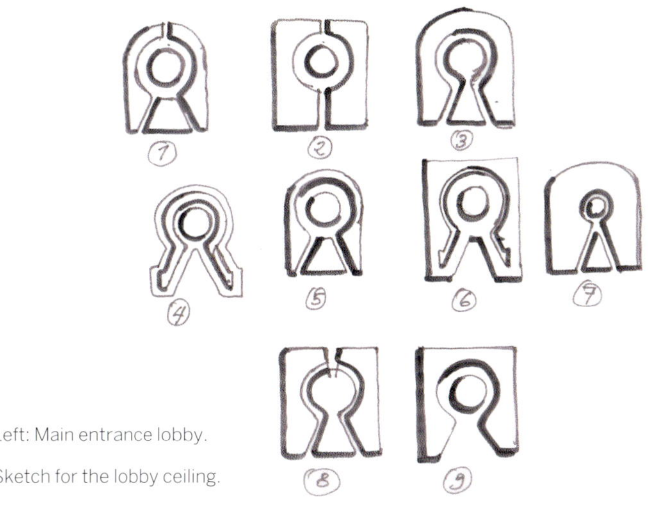

Left: Main entrance lobby.

Sketch for the lobby ceiling.

Above and right page, bottom: A bronze mirror is used in the executive office corridor to create a high ceiling effect.

Right page, top: Main entrance plan.

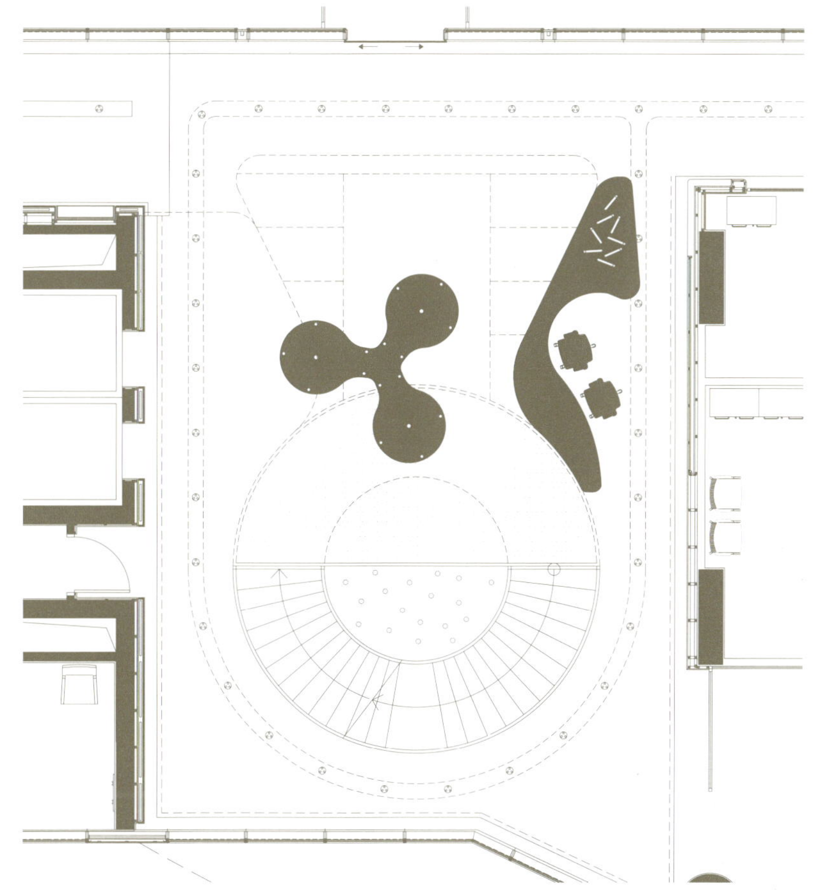

8.Kat/Floor
Yönetim Kurulu Başkanı
Chairman of the Board
Ağız ve Diş Sağlığı
Dentistry
Akupunktur
Acupuncture
Güzellik Merkezi
Beauty Center
Check-Up
Check-Up

Aspen Fair Stand 2010
33rd International Istanbul Building Fair, Istanbul, Turkey, 2010
Area: 120 m^2

Aspen is a Turkish company founded in 1989, specializing in construction materials such as ceiling and modulated partition-wall systems. Zoom/TPU was called on to design their exhibitions in 2010 and 2011 and used materials such as their metal panel ceilings, glass, and mesh. In fact, the exhibition stand was designed entirely using Aspen products. The 2010 stand adapted a very transparent or crystalline appearance with fully open sides and exhibition elements that emphasized lightness and an obvious encouragement to visitors to enter and discover the products on display in detail. Often exhibition stands have to show objects that have nothing to do with the actual stand, whereas, in this instance, the stand itself served to present the products of Aspen.

Left: A maze perception was created with the glass surfaces.

Sketch of the maze area.

Below: An interior view of the
stand, where only products of
the brand were used.

Right page, top: A general view
of the stand.
Bottom: General plan.

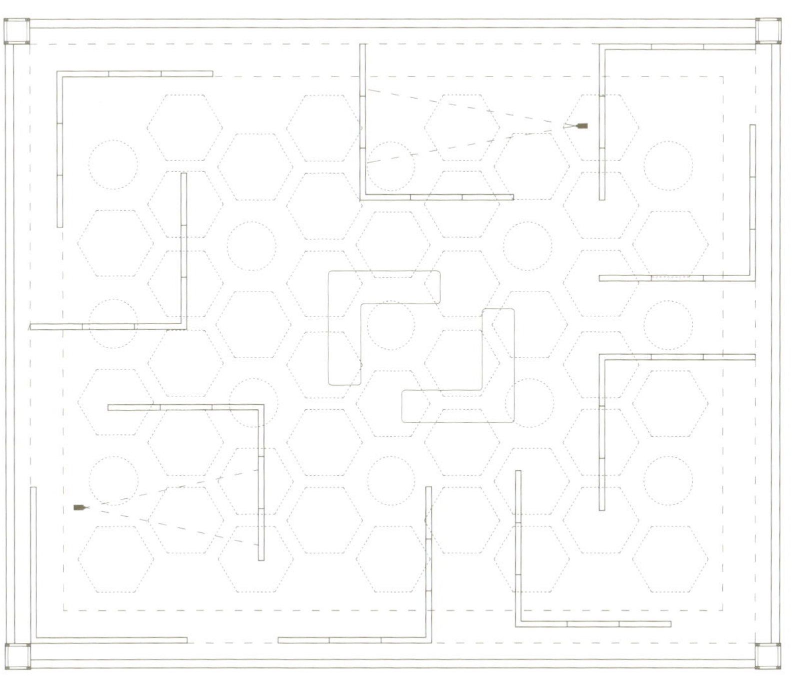

MEMORIAL

Sisli Memorial Hospital
Istanbul, Turkey, 2010
Area: 30,000 m^2

Active in areas such as organ transplants, cardiovascular surgery, cardiology, and oncology, the Sisli Memorial Hospital, also known as the Okmeydani Memorial Hospital, was founded in 1995. It has a 200-bed capacity and such features as a 120-person conference room. Zoom/TPU used solid wood panels cut with a diamond pattern as seen on many walls. Backlit stretched vinyl is used for a number of ceilings, while marble and antibacterial carpet are employed as floor cladding. The upturned glass and steel canopies at the entrance of the hospital are also the work of Zoom/TPU.

Main entrance information desk.

General views and a
sketch of the lounge area.

SALT Galata Auditorium
Istanbul, Turkey, 2011
Area: 330 m²

Located in the Beyoglu area in the European part of Istanbul, the SALT Galata project involves a non-profit cultural organization financed by the Garanti Bank. The original building with a view on the Golden Horn was the Imperial Ottoman Bank, designed by the French architect Alexandre Vallaury and built in 1872. The structure was renovated by a number of Turkish architects and designers, including Zoom/TPU for the auditorium. The former bank building now houses a museum, an exhibition space for art, an open archive for research, a library, workshops, a restaurant and office space, as well as the auditorium. Zoom/TPU explains that they participated in the effort to "restore the structure to its original state" while designing the auditorium in a "simple and contemporary way." The acoustical wooden panels employed aim to "create a resonance in time," and have forms that are inspired by sound waves.

Left page: The spotlight and the projection area were created to fit smoothly with the design of the auditorium.

Sketch of the overall area.

Following pages: General view of the auditorium showing the interpretation in wood of sound waves.

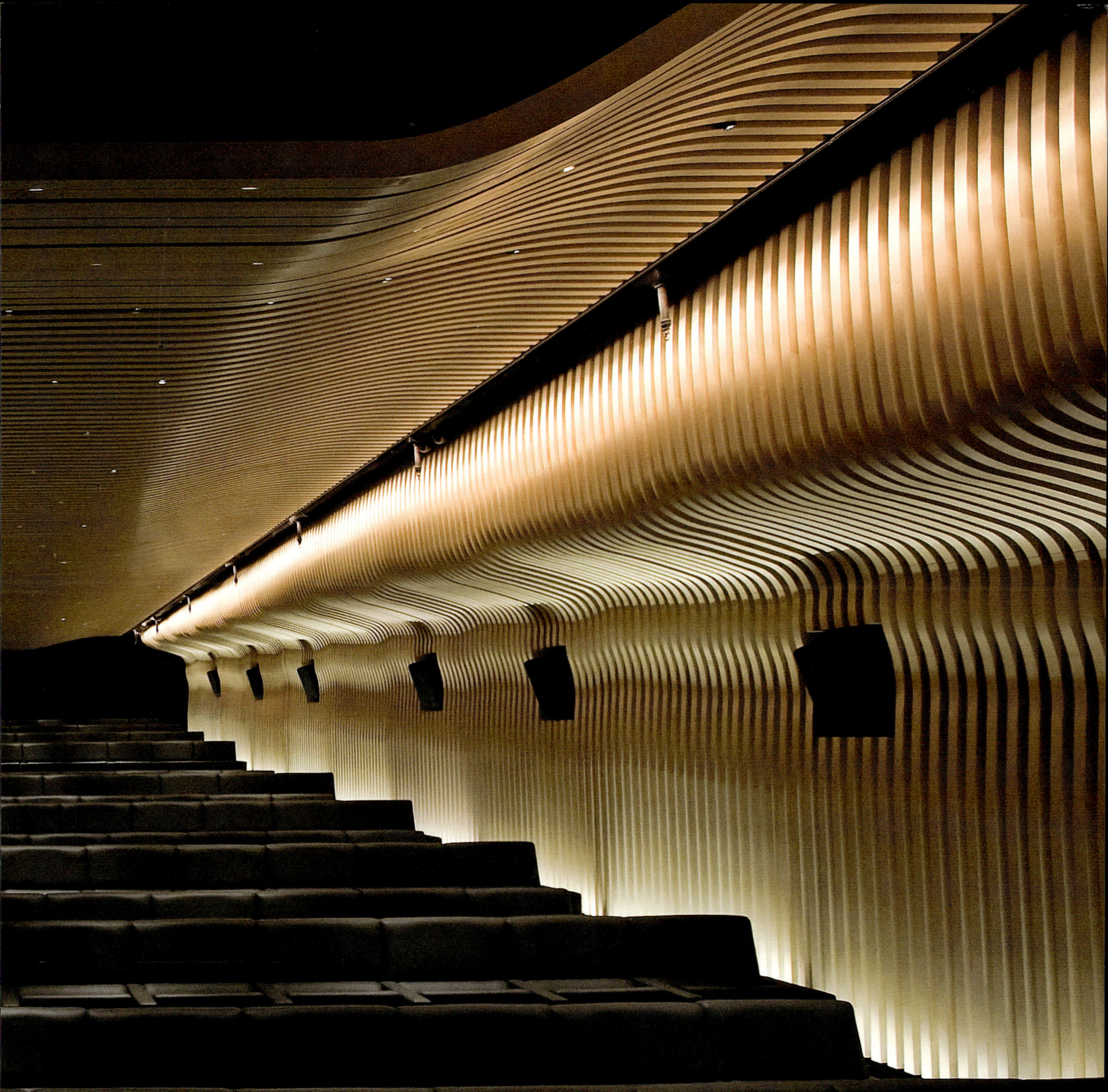

Henkel Showroom
Istanbul, Turkey, 2011
Area: 538 m^2

Amongst other businesses, the German-based firm Henkel is the world market leader in adhesives, sealants and functional coatings for consumers, craftsmen and industrial applications. Henkel began its operations in Turkey in 1963. Their Istanbul showroom is in the modern suburban area of Atasehir on the Anatolian side of the city. The designers, who used Henkel products for the ceilings and flooring, explain: "The concept is an interpretation of the group's intention to contribute to the construction chemicals sector. It is an association of colors and a material feast." Flowing surfaces, mostly colored in bright red but also sometimes marked by what looks like splatters of paint, brighten and enliven the space.

An installation showing the variations in surface effects that can be created by using the brand's own products.

Left page, top: Sketch of the safety
rail on the stairs.
Bottom: Another view showing
the variations in surface effects that
can be created by using the brand's
own products.

Above: Stairs leading
to the upstairs showroom.

Main entrance, gallery space.

Sketch of the main entrance.

Following pages: To emphasize the display and sample area, red was used for the passage.

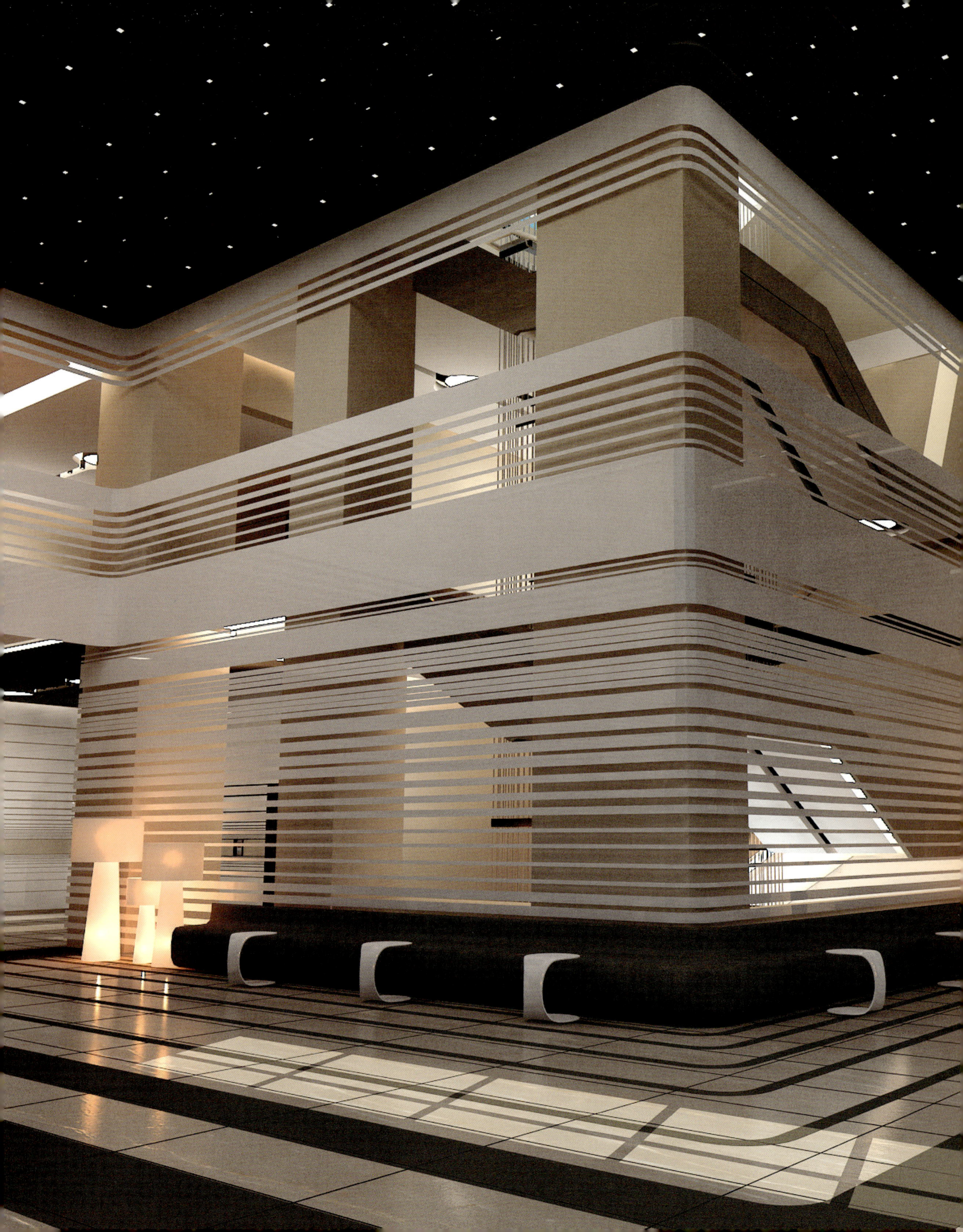

ER-PA Hospital
Denizli, Turkey, 2011
Area: 26,600 m²

Denizli is an industrial city in southwestern Turkey known for its textile industry. This is a private hospital originally founded in 1992 in the center of Denizli with eighty-two single rooms and a total capacity of 135 beds. Considered a leader in the health-care sector in Denizli, the interior of the ER-PA Hospital was designed by Zoom/TPU after extensive discussions with company management about patient behavior and expectations in a modern hospital environment. Such factors as seating arrangements and signage were taken into account. A selection of long-lasting hygienic and recyclable materials was made and Zoom/TPU deployed their usual vocabulary, using locally quarried marble, linoleum, and acrylic furniture. Translucent stairs connect the spaces of the hospital. Horizontal bands used in ceilings and floors indicate the direction visitors should take in their circulation through the building.

A glass surface creates a transparent relation between the lobby and the staircase.

Following pages: Patient corridors and nurse station.

Above: The stairs were inspired by
a bird cage.

Right page, top: Sketch of the staircase.
Bottom: Operating theatre.

ERPA HASTANESI   MERDIVEN KORKULUĞU
ETÜDÜ
11. MAR . 2013

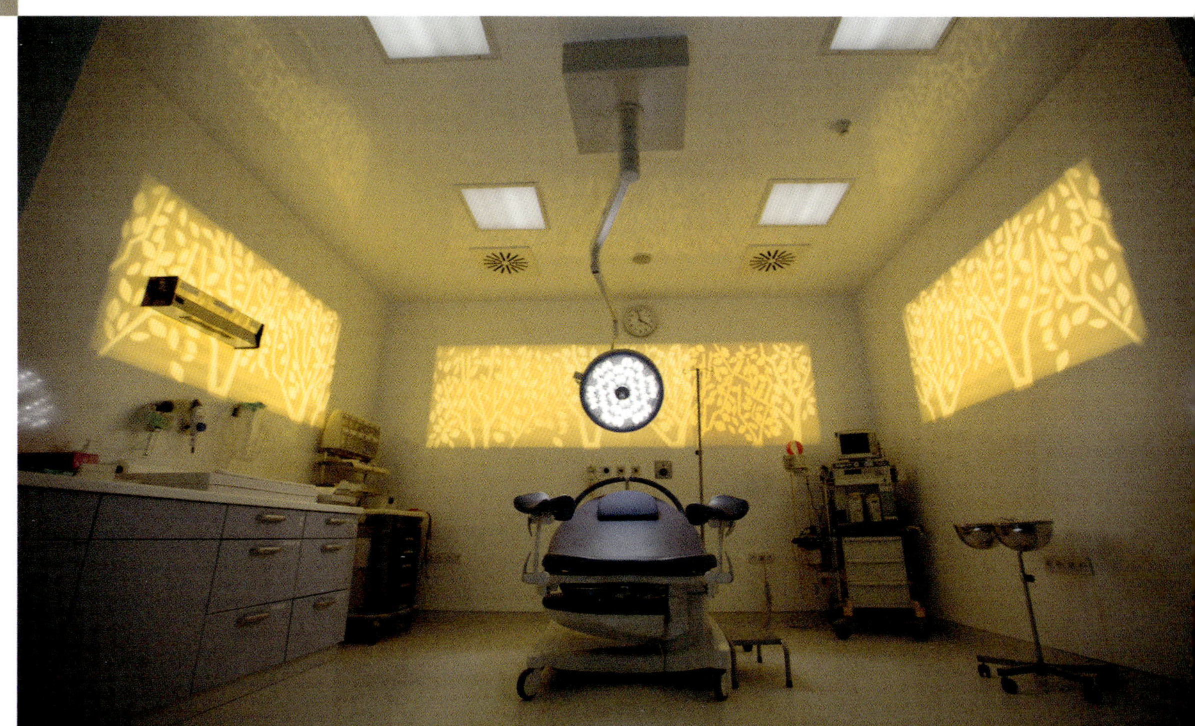

Aspen Fair Stand 2011
34th International Istanbul Building Fair, Istanbul, Turkey, 2011
Area: 120 m²

The most important aspect of the Second exhibition project of the group was the group's desire to be involved in the building sector and this was implemented with a transparent but elegant approach. Aspen and Zoom/TPU won the Altin Miknatis Best Stand Design award at YAPI-Turkeybuild (International Istanbul Building Fair) held at the Tuyap Fair Convention and Congress Center in Istanbul in both this fair in 2011 and the preceding one in 2010. An experienced jury chose the Aspen stand from amongst nearly a thousand other presentations at the Building Fair. Their criteria included the manner in which the stand emphasized and reflected the qualities of the products of Aspen and how it integrated functional and aesthetic qualities.

Left page: Entrance to the fair stand.

Sketch of the stand showing the entrance.

Below: Plan of the stand.

Right page: The honeycomb-shaped
perforated ceiling is also used as a
lighting system.

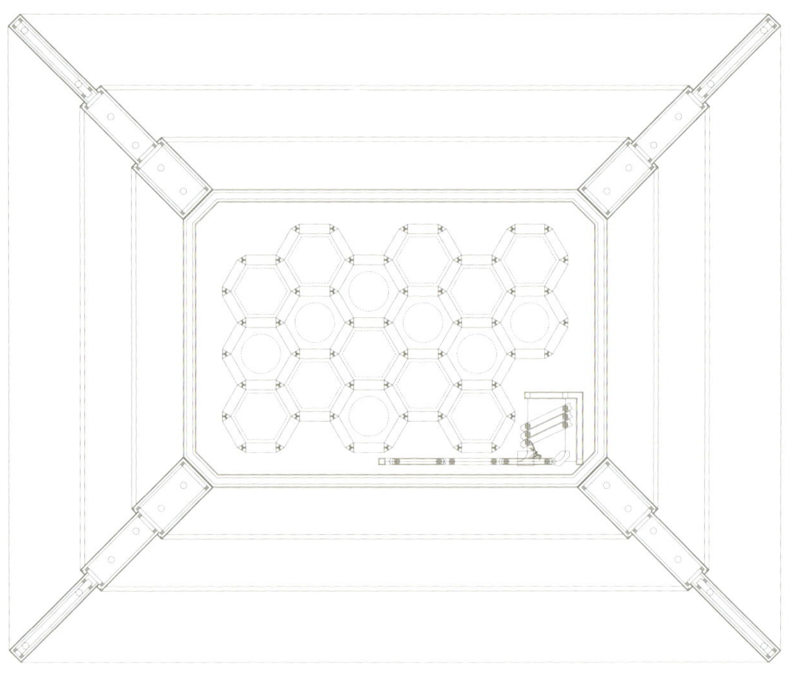

ŞERİFOĞLU
AHŞAP
LAMİNE
PARKE

Istanbul Florence Nightingale Hospital
Istanbul, Turkey, 2012
Area: 56,000 m^2

One of the five London-based Group Florence Nightingale Hospitals in Turkey, this institution is lodged in an eighteen-story structure with a heliport on the roof. The building is Turkey's first "Green Hospital Building" with a TUV Hessen Green Building Certificate. It is located in the Sisli district, on the European side of the city. There are 219 patient beds, eleven surgery rooms, and two delivery rooms. A 300-seat conference room is also part of the building. Zoom/TPU's intervention uses different materials and different approaches for the outpatient and inpatient areas. A monumental pool in the entrance and detailing intended to reflect the quality of the institution are part of the scheme.

Falling water has been used to create visual and sound effects in the two-floor lobby, which has a wide mirrored ceiling.

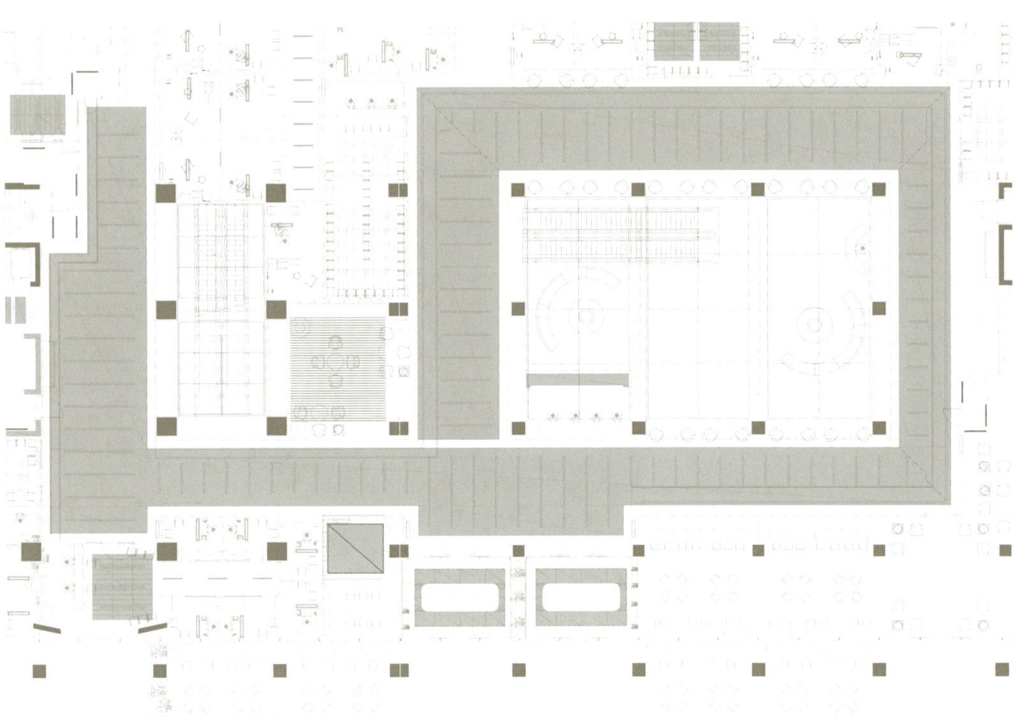

Left page: The information
desk and a plan of the lobby.

Above: A patient corridor.
Below: A patient room.

Urgan
Istanbul, Turkey, 2012
Area: 2000 m^2

Urgan is a Turkish shoe manufacturer. Zoom/TPU states: "We can say that the new office building of Urgan Ayakkabi is the beginning of new institutional identity. This approach enabled us to reevaluate the existing façade of the building and to fictionalize the relation of the façade design to the architecture." The rhythm and form of the façade are now carried through inside of the building with such elements as a three-dimensional "parametric coating" on the stairs. The interior space was fully reevaluated and the continuity of the design from the planning phase through to lighting and other aspects was taken in hand by Zoom/TPU. Marble flooring, steel and glass stairs, wood and composite acrylic wall coverings are the main materials employed by the designers.

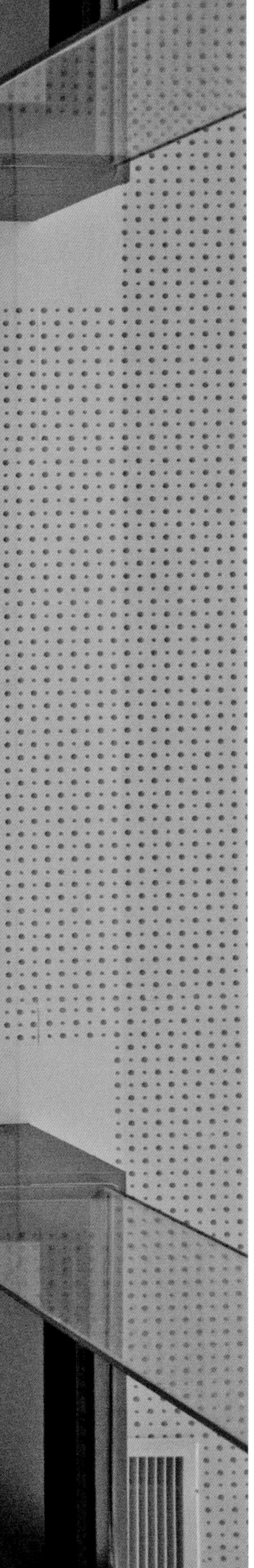

A detail showing the suspended
light hanging in the gallery space.

Below: A sketch of the lobby.

Right page: A view from the lobby
showing all floors.

Following pages 154-155: The special
patterns of the Urgan company
have been interpreted by Zoom/TPU
as a wallpaper.

Following pages 156-157: Sun-shading
devices on the façade have been used
as a design element for the exterior
of the building.

URGAN

URGAN

Ulus Liv Hospital
Istanbul, Turkey, 2012
Area: 27,987 m²

Liv Hospital was planned as one of the most innovative hospitals in the Turkish health-care sector. The institution received the American-based Joint Commission International (JCI) quality accreditation certificate shortly after its opening. With an international staff, the institution is located in the Ulus area on the European side of Turkey's largest city. Zoom/TPU explains: "The distinctive factor of the design concept was a hygiene-oriented focus and how we could interpret the cult science-fiction movie *Fantastic Voyage*, which depicts the human body." The designers worked in close collaboration not only with the Liv Clinic group, but also with manufacturers to obtain the obviously careful detailing seen in the hospital. Working their ideas about the *Fantastic Voyage* theme, Zoom/TPU developed a "geometry of organic forms" that was "applied to the architectural structure as a visual theme." They go on to state: "A futuristic atmosphere and environment was created within the awareness that people should feel safe and welcome in a hospital where they usually feel the most vulnerable." Zoom/TPU refers to the "struggle in nature to soften the sharp edges," another idea that surely drove their very complete and nearly "seamless" design. Functional conduits (heating, electricity, and so on) are hidden in patient corridors with an aluminum ceiling net, while LED lighting guides visitors and patients alike inside the building. This project was a finalist in the 2011 World Architecture Festival Awards.

Cafeteria and lounge areas.

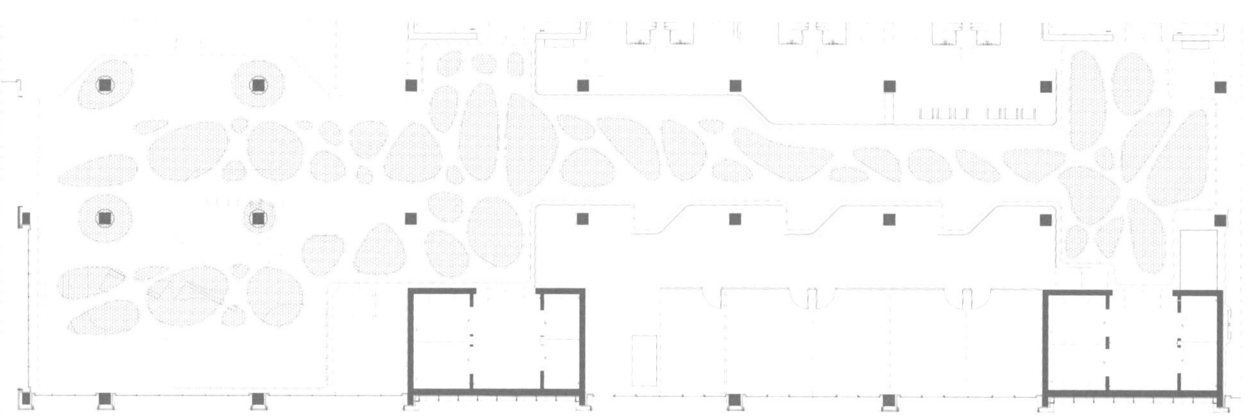

Above: Another view of the cafeteria and lounge areas.

Left: Schematic plan of the main entrance ceiling.

The information desk at the
entrance also refers to the
human body and organic forms,
as does the rest of the interior.

Waiting rooms in the polyclinic areas.

An executive patient examination room.

Emergency observation rooms.

Below: Nurse station.

Following pages: The information desk
and the waiting lounge seating system
organically complete each other.

Zoom/TPU Office
Istanbul, Turkey, 2012
Area: 300 m^2

Located in the Beyoglu/Taksim district in Istanbul, the Zoom/TPU offices have a generous ceiling height, and the approach of the designers to their own workspace was to be "unpretentious, respectable, and peaceful." Wood surfaces and wood parquet are juxtaposed with some epoxy flooring, with an "exposed concrete effect" for the jack arches. Existing stone walls in the old building had to be protected, but Zoom/TPU added touches of color as well as a varied palette of materials to create a modern feeling in the space.

Atilla Kuzu's work desk.

Following pages: The entrance and welcome desk of the office, and a meeting room.

ZOOM/TPU

A sketch and view of the corridor,
where the original roof paneling
has been maintained.

LOSEV Facility
Ankara, Turkey, 2013–ongoing
Area: 130,000 m^2

LOSEV, The Foundation for Children with Leukemia, which is a non-profit NGO, was founded in 1998. The institution wishes to expand its reach and even the age limits of its clientele. Located in a popular residential district of Ankara, the facility seeks to provide children with social facilities and other amenities not often found in this context. A hotel is mainly for the relatives of patients. One of the most extensive hospital facilities of its type, LOSEV aims to open its new spaces, designed by Zoom/TPU, in late 2015. As usual, the design is based on extensive conversations with the directors of the institution and can be called an interpretation of their goals. Zoom/TPU states: "The design symbolizes the presence of the foundation in Turkey. Even more than other hospital projects, this one is based on the foundation's specific and clearly expressed wishes. Zoom/TPU has once again used its inviting style that encourages healing, but in a more colorful way." An original design proposed a school for patients to be included in the complex, but this idea has evolved and as this book went to press the possibility of creating an actual university as part of the project was being considered.

The hotel reception desk

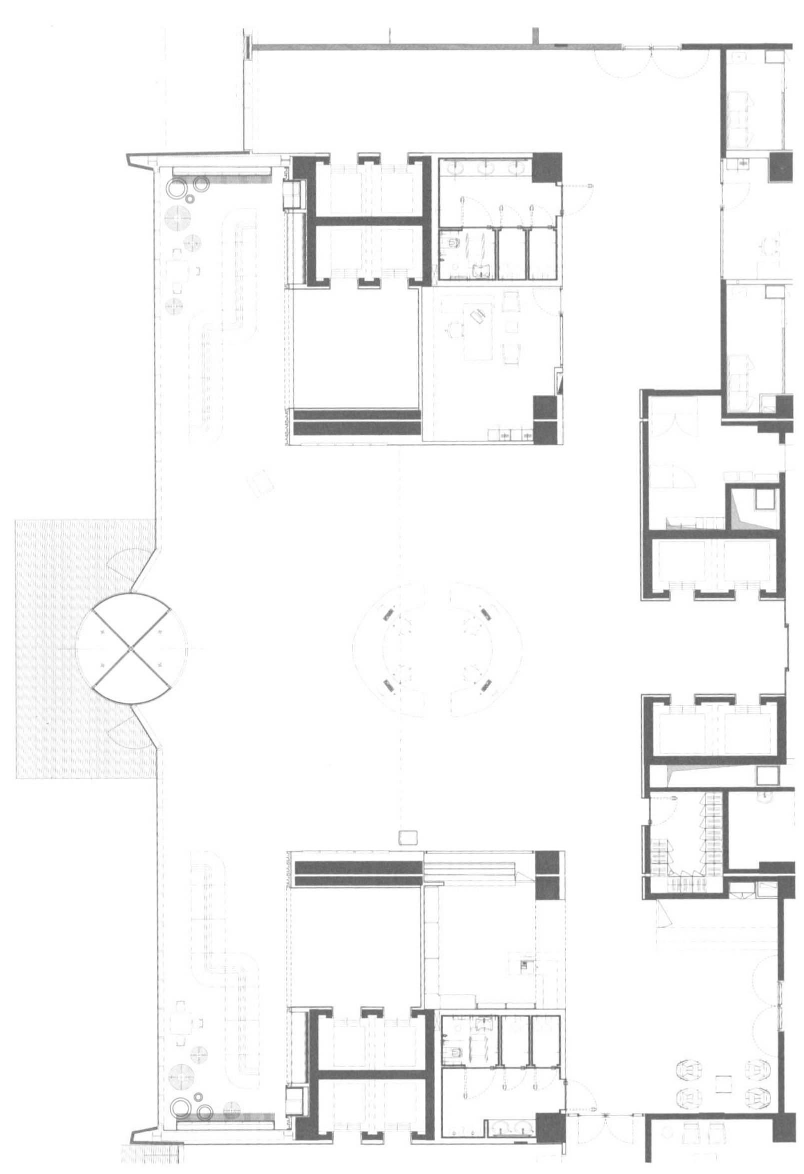

The School

Above: Plan of the main
entrance of the hospital block.

Right page, above: Corridor
with wall surfaces that children
can write on and then erase.
Below: A typical classroom
with acoustic ceiling.

1A
B
A

The Hotel

Above: A standard room.

Right page: Corridor.

The Hospital
Above: Oncology entrance lounge.

Right page: A corridor in the polyclinic
and an executive patient room.

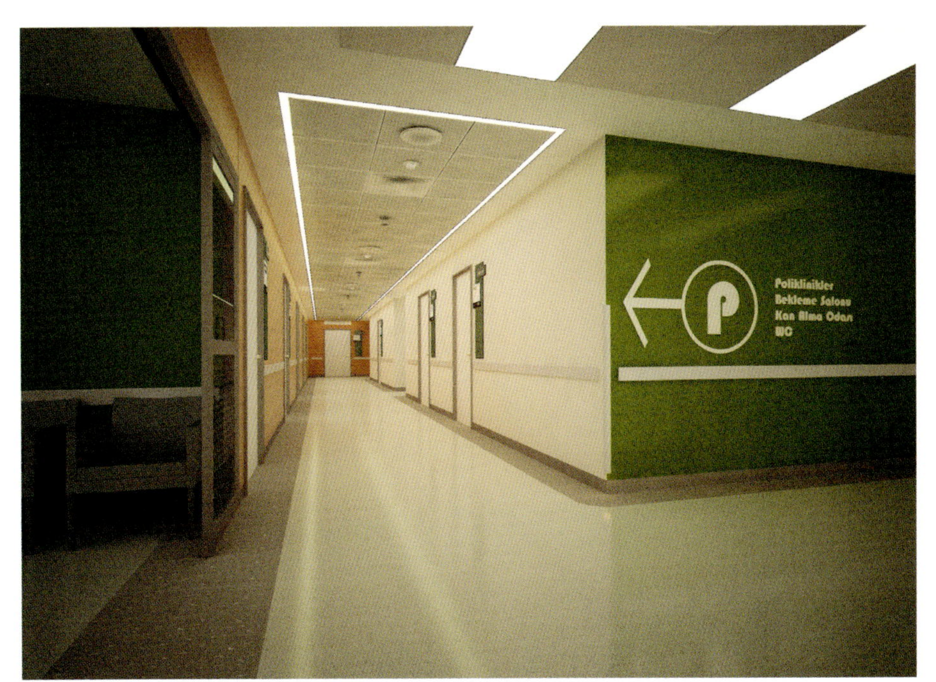

P
Poliklinikler
Bekleme Salonu
Kan Alma Odası
WC

Hill-Rom.

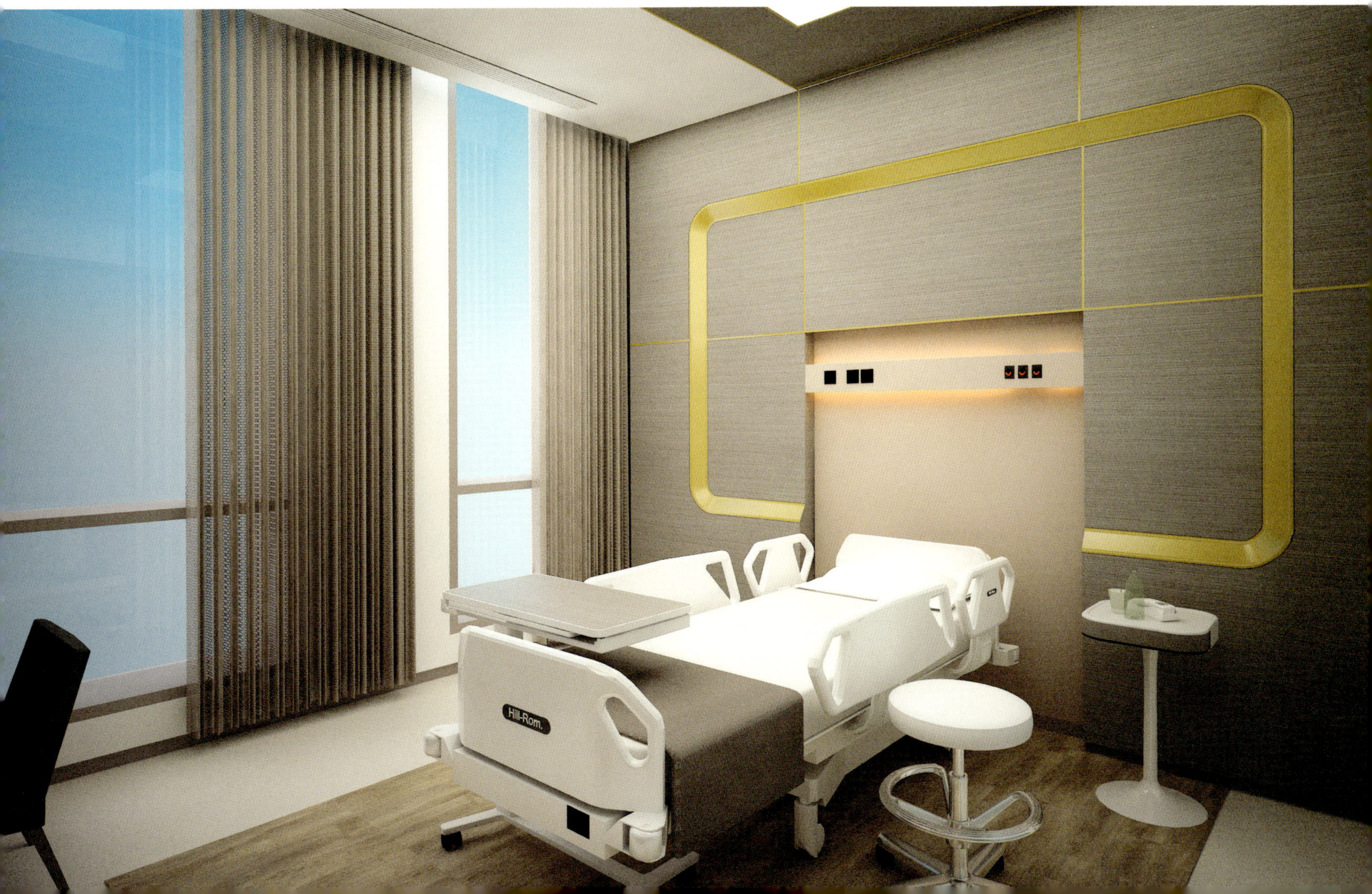

Ankara Memorial Hospital
Ankara, Turkey, 2013
Area: 30,989 m^2

The 230-bed Ankara Memorial Hospital is one of ten institutions controlled by the Memorial Healthcare Group. Located on the Konya Highway, the facility allows easy access from the city for local patients but also for foreigners. Again, originally planned as an office building, this structure had to be completely redesigned by Zoom/TPU. They state: "First we re-planned all stairs, shafts, entrances, exits, and circulation schemes. Thematically oriented light patterns on ceilings guide visitors through spaces where hygienic materials are used for floors and walls." Painted glass, marble, and ceramics are combined with decorative plexiglas ceiling panels. Open cells in the ceilings allow mechanical and electrical systems to be placed out of sight, maintaining the very smooth flow of all the surfaces and furnishings, also designed by Zoom/TPU.

View from the main entrance.

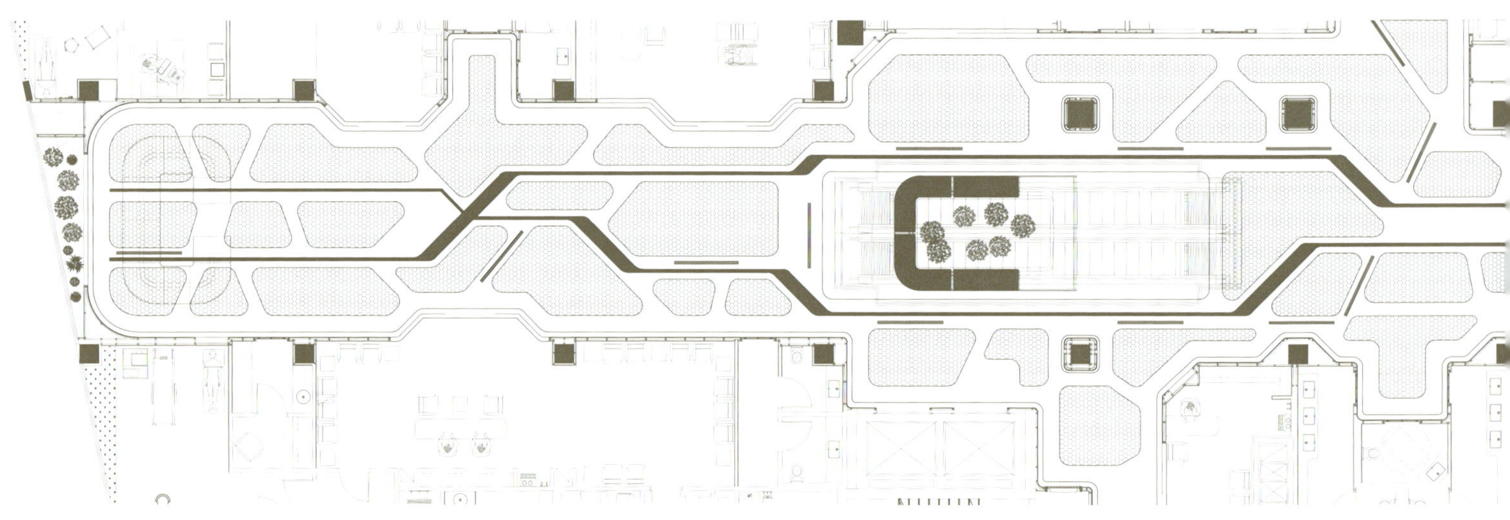

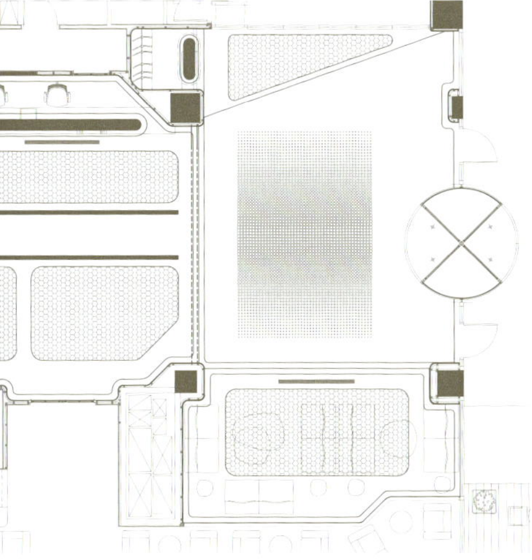

Above: Transparent polyclinic areas.

Left: Main entrance lobby plan.

Sketch of an alternative patient room
and a standard patient room with
graphic detailing at the head of the bed.

Right page: Standard patient corridor
and the information desk showing a
detail that enhances disabled access.

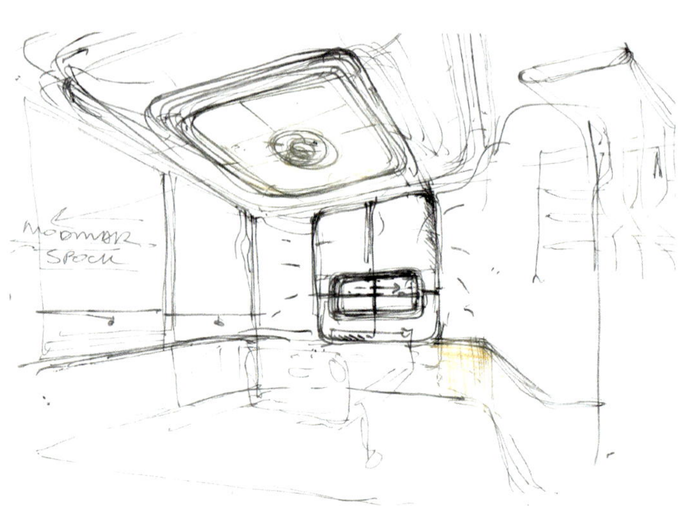

CHECK-UP

Below: Sketches of the information
and appointment desks.

Right page: Executive patient corridor.

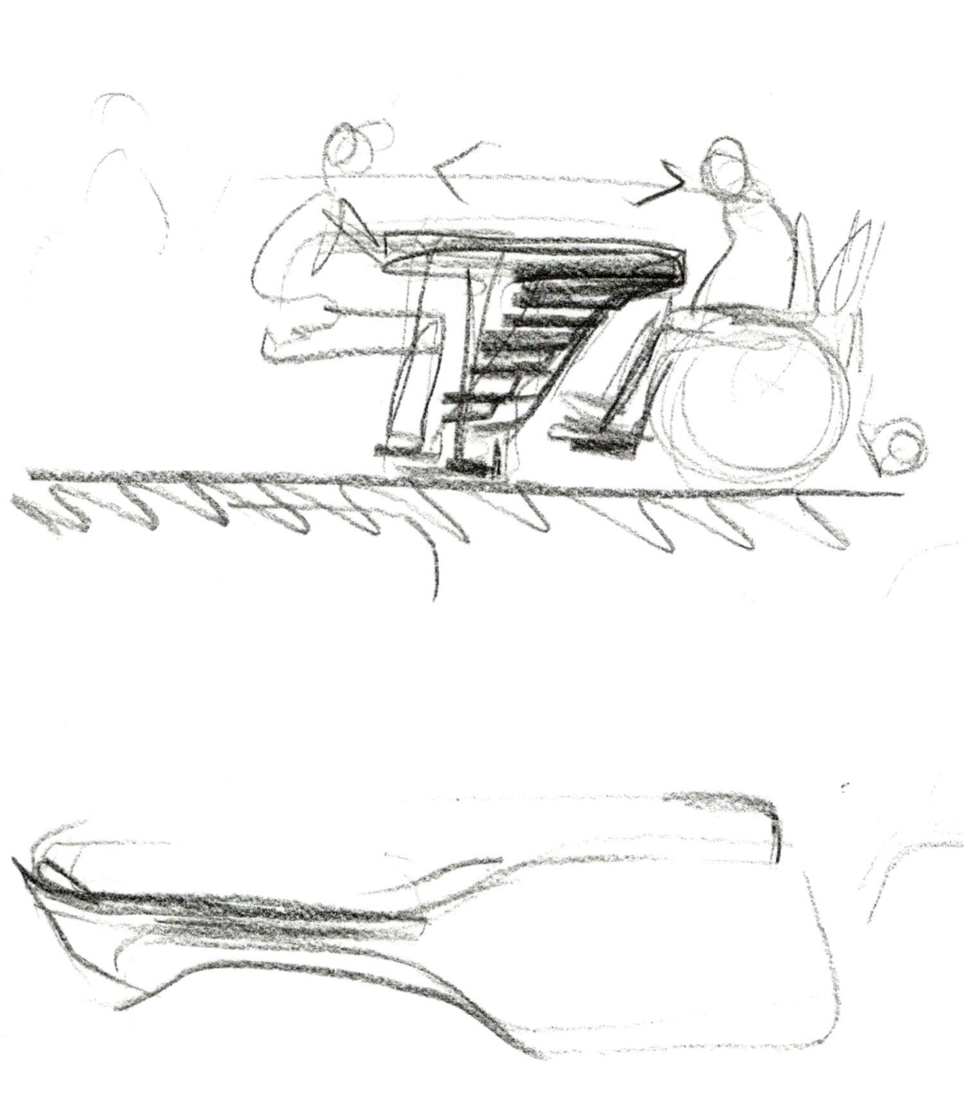

9.
KAT/FLOOR
1907
1908
1906
1909
1905
1910
1904
1911
1903
1901
1902

TR-Pharm
Istanbul, Turkey, 2013
Area: 587 m^2

TR-Pharm is "an R&D-based innovative company established to offer alternatives for certain treatments." Their headquarters is located in the Kanyon complex located in the Levent and designed in 2006 by the Istanbul architects Tabanlioglu. Zoom/TPU was called to design the offices of TR-Pharm on the fourteenth floor of the Kanyon building. They employed a parametric pattern that gives a three-dimensional impression for the flooring. In almost all parts of the office, concealed lighting and ceiling spotlights create a homogenous light level. A honeycomb design with holes was used for the ceiling. All of the office units, from that of the chairman to meeting rooms and open office space, were designed with an intention to create an overall harmony. Zoom/TPU designed not only the overall office space in this instance, but also tables for the chairman, meeting tables, and wall units for books or televisions. Zoom/TPU emphasizes that "from beginning to end, the TR-Pharm project was very exciting and enjoyable for us, and it was particularly satisfying to work not only on the design but also on its practical application."

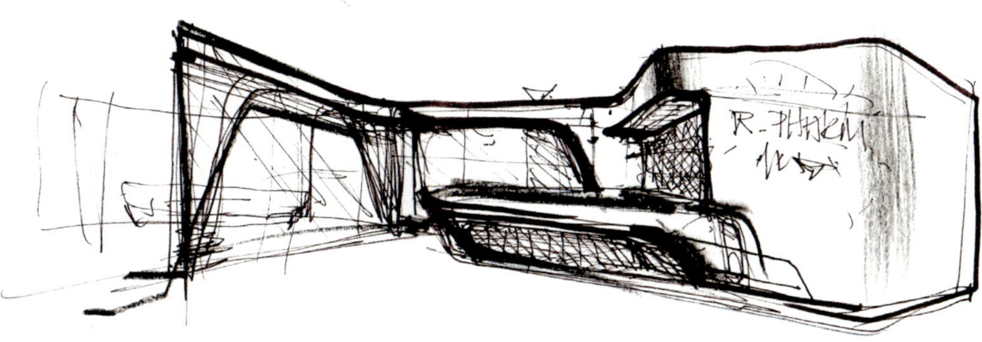

A view and an early sketch of the main entrance with a flying desk and 3D carpet effect.

Left page, top: The open office system offers an option for flexibility. Bottom: General schematic plan.

Below: A meeting room with parametric-design ceilings and bookshelf details.

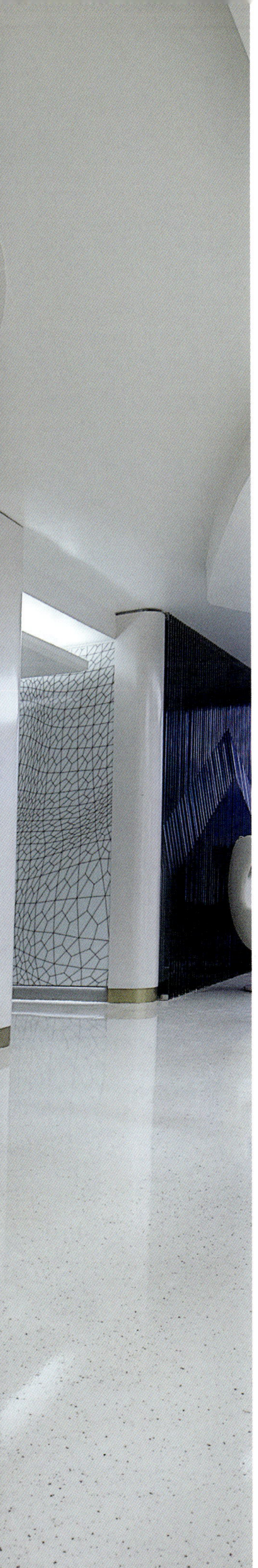

Zorlu Memorial Clinic
Istanbul, Turkey, 2013
Area: 255 m^2

Located in Mecidiyekoy on the European side of Istanbul, this clinic was planned by Zoom/TPU in a spirit of "organic and sculptural liquidity." Surfaces do indeed flow into each other, creating a very obvious continuity in the spaces. Mirrors, marble, ceramics, laminate-coated MDF, gypsum-board ceilings, acrylic furniture, and a stretched vinyl ceiling with open cells all contribute to the material aspects of the space, which is meant to be "calm and impressive" according to the designers. Generous open spaces and furnishings that are quite literally integrated into the design contribute to making patients and those who accompany them feel at ease in a very modern, technically sophisticated atmosphere.

Reception desk with rounded detailing.

Below: A parametric pattern
created by Zoom/TPU to somewhat
dissimulate the transparency.

Right page: Fluid design seating
units and a general view.

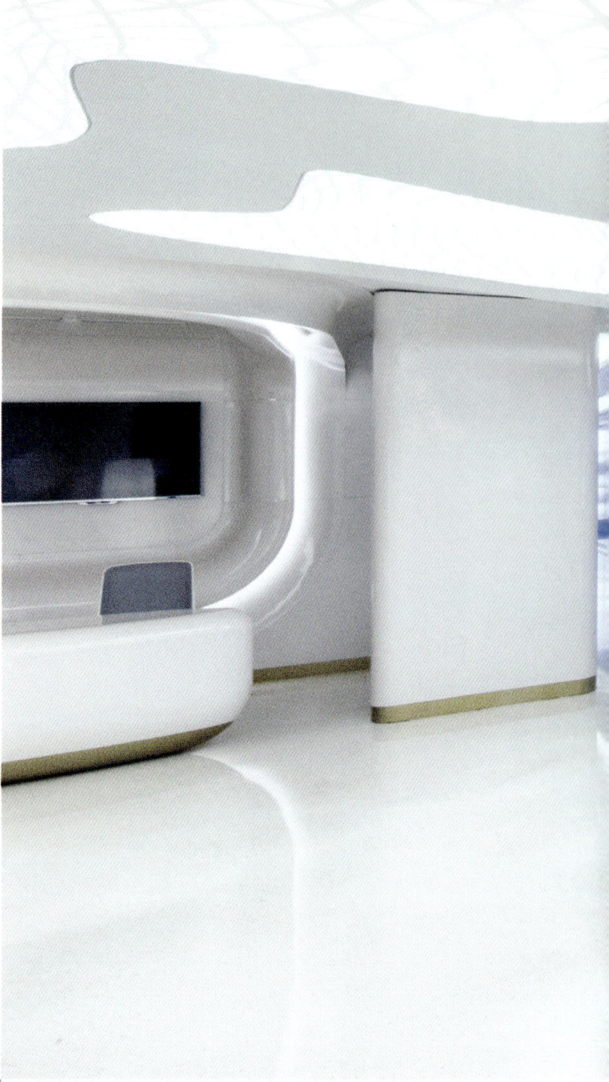

A sketch and a view along the corridor.

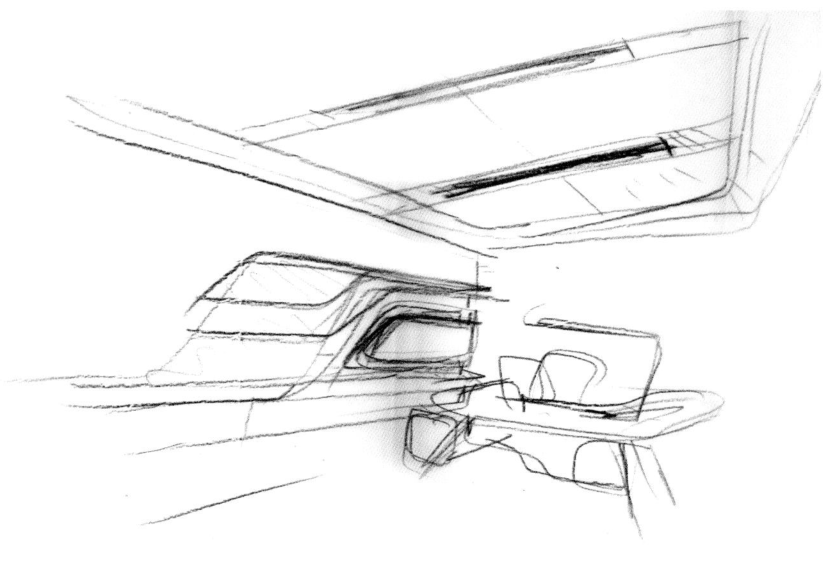

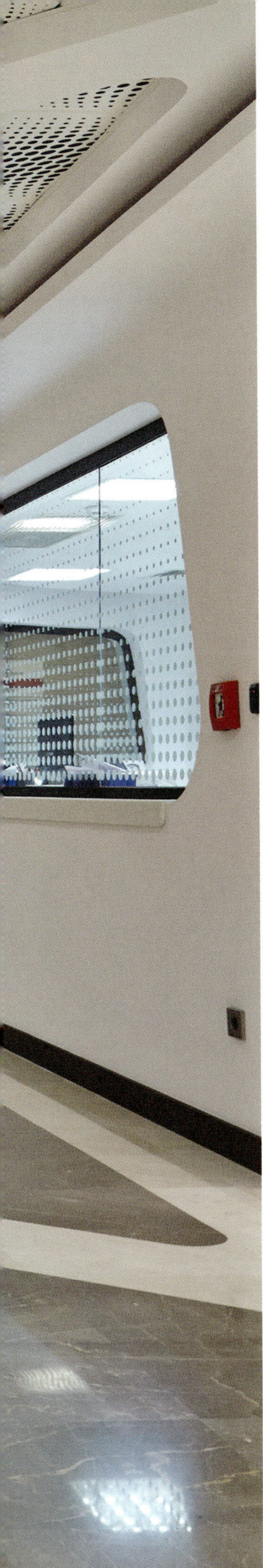

Kolan Hospital
Istanbul, Turkey, 2013
Area: 18,652 m²

This project was carried out in a period of one year for the Kolan Health Group, which was founded in 1997, and aims for the highest international standards in health care. Making use of mirrored ceilings, marble for the floors of the lobby and patient bathrooms, ceramics in wet areas, laminate-coated MDF on the walls of the clinic corridors, gypsum-board ceilings, acrylic furniture, and modular perforated metal ceilings in patient corridors and the lobby, Zoom/TPU has given a very coherent and comprehensible design to this 173-bed facility. Planted areas punctuate the more public spaces, serving to alleviate the rather smooth continuity of the overall design, and enable patients to see something other than the pure hospital environment.

Waiting lounge with
visible laboratory areas.

Below: The emergency entrance.

Right page: A typical patient room
and the plan of the emergency entrance.

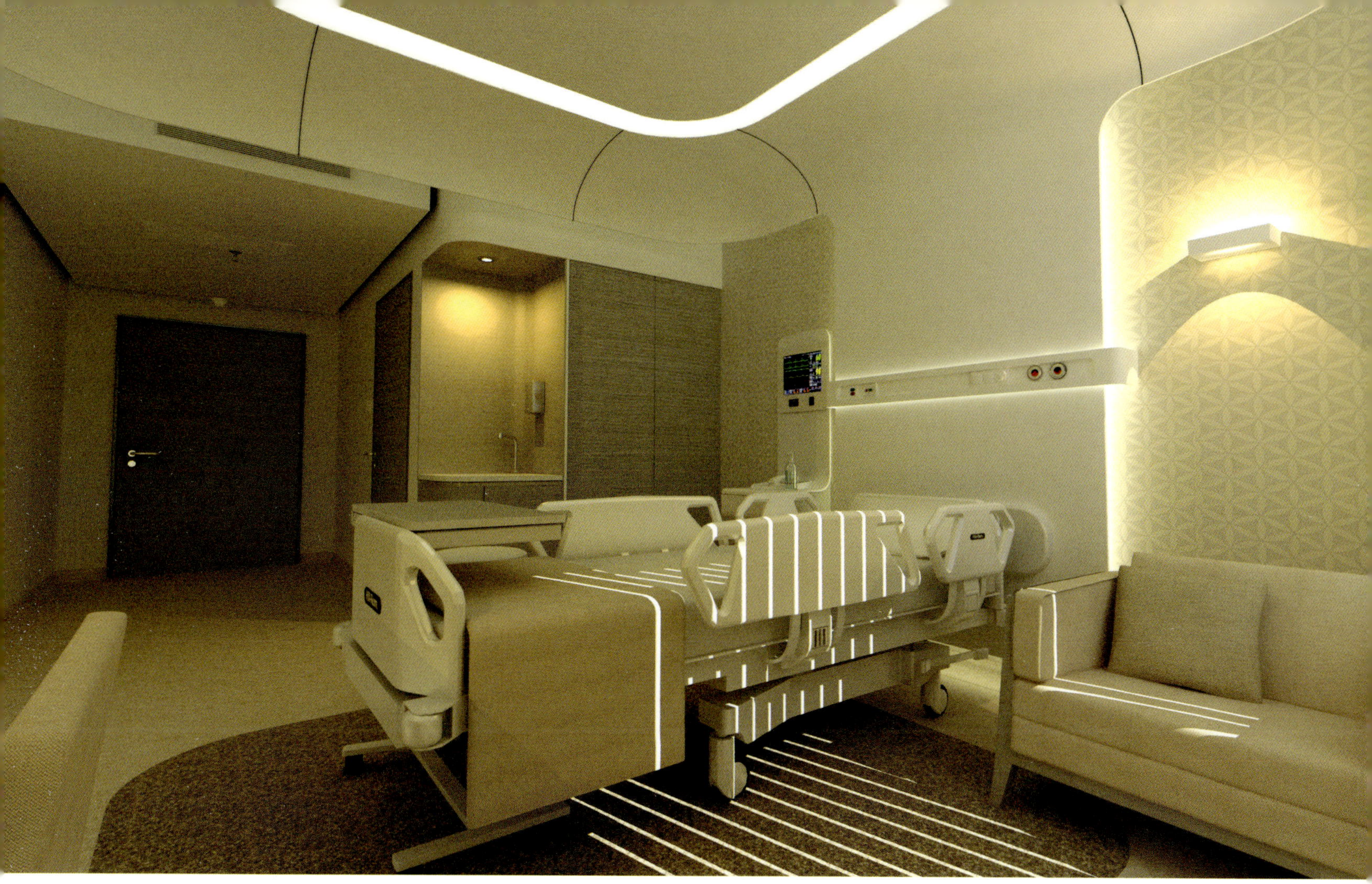

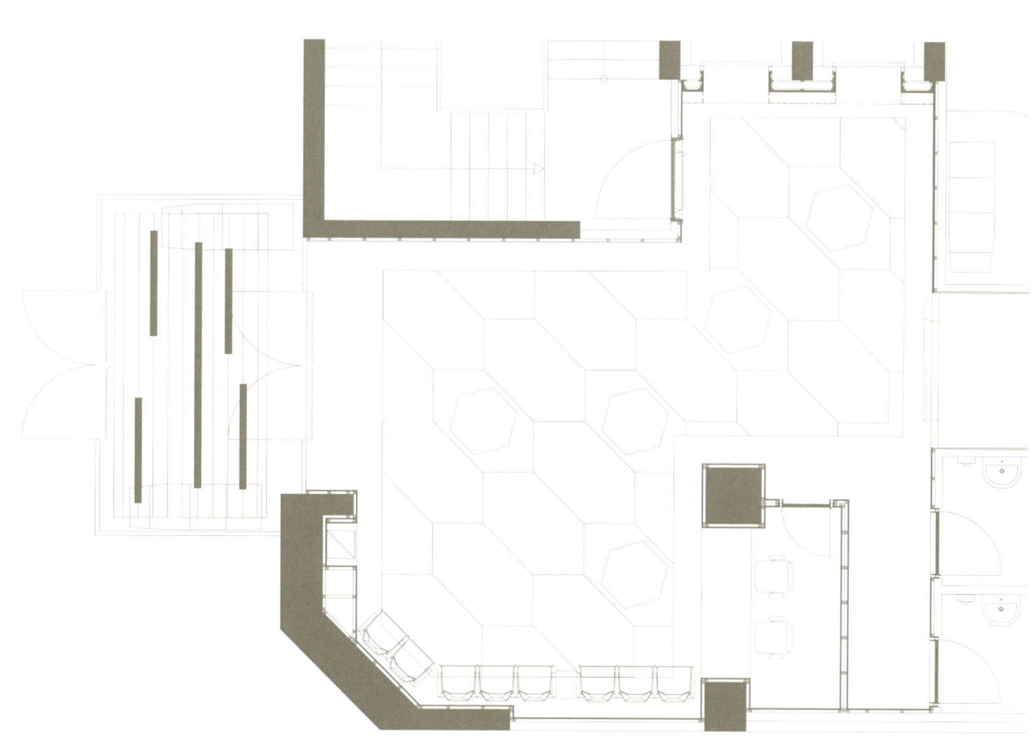

Ankara Liv Hospital
Ankara, Turkey, 2014
Area: 15,000 m²

For this project, Zoom/TPU was called on to transform an office building into a hospital. The institution is located in the Cankaya area of the Turkish capital, near the administrative heart of the hospital. The design emphasizes the concept of contact with the outside world, from sun coming through the window, to the sound of birds. This contact with the exterior is meant to be the point where healing begins. The immune system of the human body is used as a source of inspiration, in particular, in this instance, the presence of white and red blood cells in the battle against illness. A terrazzo coating is used for the lobby, while the textures and movements of the gypsum-board ceiling emphasize the metaphor of the immune system. Acrylic is used as an essential material in patient rooms and bathrooms. Acrylic is also used in the patient rooms for turquoise mirrors. For the bathrooms, one of the natural materials—marble—has been used, together with the acrylic. Marble and wood-textured patchwork wallpaper in the patient rooms add a warm touch as well as being attractive innovative materials in this context. The dental clinic differs from the other spaces with its customized instruments; it is detailed in harmony with its function but remains in the spirit of the rest of the design.

Lobby with soft colors, fluid furniture,
and terracotta cladding details.

Above: A patient corridor.

Right page, top: A sketch
and detail of the corridor.
Bottom: The information
desk and waiting lounge.

Medical gases have been camouflaged by the sliding glass panels at the side of the bed.

An examination room.

RECEPTION

Karakoy Hotel
Istanbul, Turkey, design 2014
Area: 2400 m^2

The Karakoy Hotel project was originally a restoration/transformation of the Hovagimyan Han. "Han" means "little Ottoman caravanserai-khan" in Turkish. There are many khans located in this historic district of Istanbul. Karakoy was also a port and trade center for many years. The Hovagimyan Han was built by the Armenian architect Levon Nafilyan in the 1920s in an Art Nouveau style. The planned hotel has fifty rooms along with a two-floor restaurant. Zoom/TPU's approach consisted in preserving the original design without many basic changes in the character of the structure. Electrical wiring, for example, is placed along walls in pipes instead of being embedded in the walls. Electrical and mechanical systems are also visible in the restaurant for the same reason. Ceilings are covered with porous materials such as mesh. A plaster that looks like concrete was added, while the original wall textures of the structure were preserved. Natural materials such as wood, parquet, and marble are used in the hotel. Room design, with detailing like pipes and mesh, are harmonious with the public spaces. With this design concept Zoom/TPU tried to bring out the beauties of the original historic structure without adding too many ornaments or other extraneous components. This concept project is not to be built.

The reception desk shows Zoom/TPU's style used in a historical building.

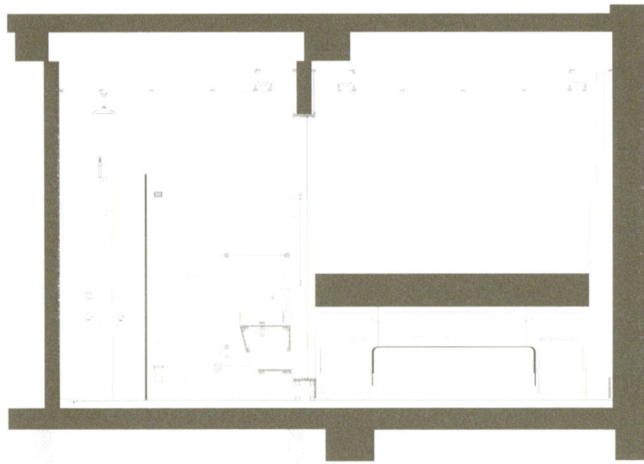

Left page, top: Light and copper colors have been used with the industrial atmosphere of the rooms. Bottom: Section of a room.

Above: Transparency is emphasized in the relation between the room, bathroom, dressing room, and wardrobe. Below: The cable systems are carried by copper pipes used as a design element.

Indirect, homogeneous light
has been used in the corridors,
staircases, and signage.

The historical aspects of the
building have been conserved
in the restaurant by using copper
material and concrete columns.

Erciyes Hotel
Kayseri, Turkey, design 2014
Area: 10,000 m²

This ambitious project was designed entirely by Zoom/TPU at the request of two well-known investors who wanted to attract weekend visitors or business clients. It took into account the location of the project in both geographical and demographic terms. The requirement to function in all four seasons, and the desire to use local textures and materials were amongst the challenges faced by the designers. Zoom/TPU proposed a traditional roof that is derived from regional shingled designs and used local Erciyes marble as well as other materials that can be readily found in the vicinity for their proposal. Feasibility studies unfortunately showed that the expected tourist flows in the area are not sufficient and that implementation of the construction also posed problems, so the project is on hold. Mount Erciyes (3916 m) is the tallest mountain in Anatolia, and draws many tourists for skiing. The hotel is located near Mount Erciyes and was designed with a respect for the characteristic slopes of the mountain. The forty-two-room hotel was designed with a main restaurant, a fine-dining facility, and à la carte restaurant, as well as a health club, spa, and children's space.

A warm and cozy atmosphere has been created with lighting and furniture details for this hotel located in a winter resort area.

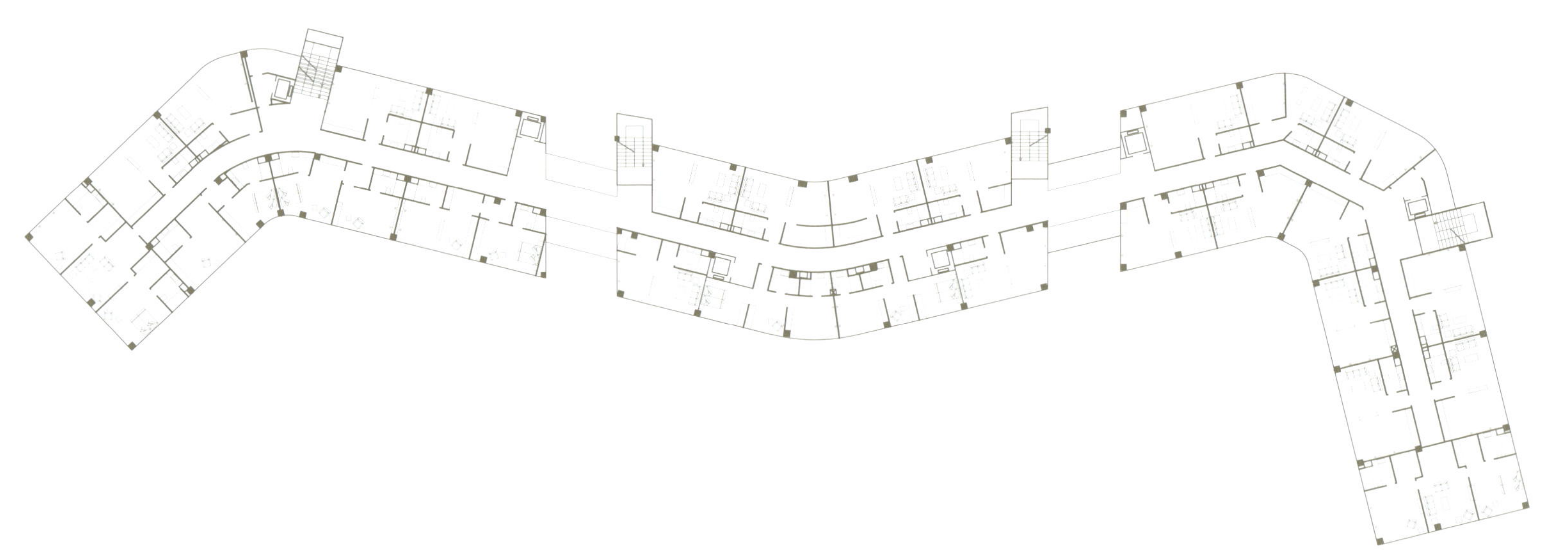

Left page, top: The front façade shows a combination of local materials with steel construction and glass elements. Bottom: A typical room floor plan.

Below: The lounge area.

Following pages: To emphasize contrasts, create a feeling of warmth and dissipate any hint of isolation, the latest technology (the LED screens for example) has been used along with the natural wooden block welcome counter.

PROF. DR.
RABIA AYDIN

Avrasya Hospital
Istanbul, Turkey, 2014–ongoing
Area: 30,000 m²

The exterior of the Avrasya Hospital project emphasizes the healing process by using color tones ranging from dark to light. In the lobby, it is possible to see objects with the OZON brand-name created by Zoom / TPU. The coffee table called Alfa Alfa and the seating design are pieces from OZON's collection specially selected for this project. The ceiling lights symbolize white blood cells that are main elements of the human immune system. In the patients' rooms it is again possible to see the story of the healing process symbolized by color tones, except that this time the colors range from light shades lower down that become darker higher up, signifying the disappearance of illness from the patient. In the patient and examination rooms, the information system's exaggerated size is used as a graphic tool; the use of graphic displays is a significant factor in this project. The hospital consists of ninety-four standard patient rooms, forty-four examination rooms, and seven operating rooms.

Built-in seating and graphic,
door signage details characterize
the polyclinic corridors.

Left page: The lower-floor entrance
showing the wide three-floor
gallery space and a sketch of the
lower-floor lobby.

Below: The lighting and canopy
detail emphasize the lower entrance.

Gentas Fair Stand
38th International Istanbul Building Fair, Istanbul, Turkey, 2015
Area: 280 m²

This fair stand is unusual for a number of reasons. The designers have emphasized "sculptural" forms and a colorful, layered appearance. One of the challenges was to build the entire stand at the 38th YAPI-Turkeybuild (International Istanbul Building Fair) with the products of Gentas, one of the world's largest producers of laminates, and the largest in Turkey. While making use of the laminate products of Gentas, Zoom/TPU succeeded in imposing their own design language. Gentas also produces metal frames for tables, chairs, and school furniture, including school desks, teacher's desks, blackboards, student's lockers, stools, benches, and seat/seat backs, as well as desks and chairs for amphitheaters. The parametric design used here is related to the firm's new stadium chair and extends to the shapes of the stand itself, including the wall, floor, and information desk. The desk leads smoothly to stairs that connect the ground and upper levels. Both the stairs and the desk are inspired by the curves found in naturally eroded canyons. The upstairs space was created in part for the needs of visitors, including a private meeting area. Closed office space and a service area are also on the upper level.

The new product and color chart details of the brand have been reproduced on the wall to create a textured effect.

Left: The exterior of the stand.
Below: A similar color scheme
has been chosen from the brand
products to create an overall nuance
of tones at the point of the stairs.

Above: The flexibility of the material
is emphasized in the columns.

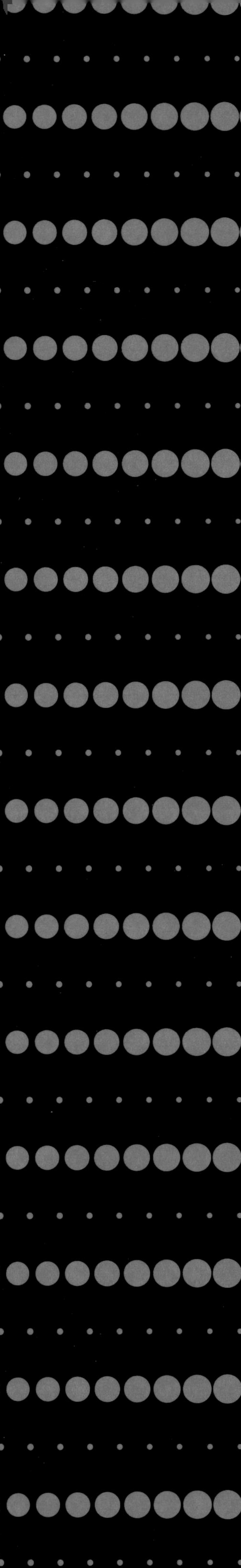

The Practice

The American philosopher and Marxist humanist writer Marshall Berman wrote *All That Is Solid Melts Into Air*. The title of this 1982 book can well describe the working system of the Zoom/TPU office, since there are no solid internal boundaries in the relationships between the partners and the co-workers. In fact, the Zoom/TPU system could be described as organic and flexible, yet very consistent.

Two groups work on the projects: one is responsible for design while the other is the project team. The design group is coordinated by the interior designer Yunus Emre Kara, who creates the concepts, while the project group is coordinated by the architect Ozge Berberoglu Kurbak, who brings these concepts to life. Each group member is responsible for the details of the entire project, with a high degree of responsibility. Zoom/TPU has always encouraged teamwork, and this method has developed over the years.

The outstanding capabilities of each team member are clearly a valuable element for the firm and encouraging these skills is one of the main goals of the organization. Research, development and education are very important parts of the system. Instead of dividing their power, they combine their skills and create an effective synergy.

Brainstorming sessions in which team members are encouraged to express themselves freely are organized on a regular basis. The way team members talk, how they dress, how they decorate the office, how their drawing and writing looks, their personalities, hobbies and dreams… all of these details express the same language as their design, and reflect their philosophy. They are creating a "Zoom/TPU culture" in their own habitat, and try to spread these values while expressing this culture in design details. A vision that is nourished by the Zoom/TPU culture is being created for each and every project.

Zoom/TPU creates new experiences in every one of its projects and offers a new life style that it wishes to emphasize in each project.

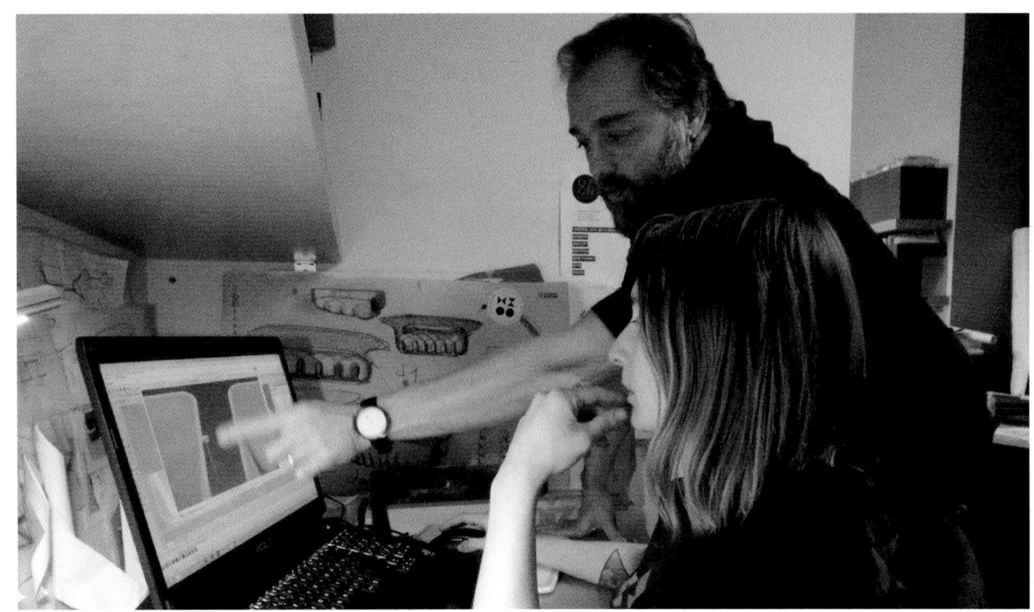

This innovative approach combines with employers' experiences.

The team is very young and includes architects, interior architects and product designers, as well as research and development people. The co-workers grow together and learn from each other. They evolve together along with the partners of Zoom/TPU, Atilla Kuzu and Levent Cirpici.

Marshall Berman, *All That Is Solid Melts Into Air: The Experience of Modernity*, Simon & Schuster, New York, 1982.

Appendix

Project Credits

Acibadem Clinic
Category: Hospital
Year: 2004
Client: APY
Electrical Planning: Akademi
Electrical Installation: Akademi
Mechanical Planning: Akademi
Static Strengthening: Yusuf Ozkan

Afrodit Exclusive
Category: Retail
Year: 2006
Client: Erkan Kantarci

Pierre Cardin Osmanbey
Category: Retail
Year: 2006
Client: Aydin Textile
Electrical Planning:
Aydin Textile Construction Group
Mechanical Planning:
Aydin Textile Construction Group

Bursa Acibadem Hospital
Category: Hospital
Year: 2006
Client: APY
Architectural Planning:
Ertunga Architectural Office
Electrical Planning: APY
Electrical Installation: APY
Mechanical Planning: APY
Static Engineers: APY

Derimod Capacity
Category: Retail
Year: 2007
Client: Zerrin Zaim, Umit Zaim
Architectural Consultant:
Chapman Taylor
Architectural Planning: Muammer Bakir

Electrical Planning:
Derimod Technical Department
Mechanical Planning:
Derimod Technical Department

**Yesilkoy Acibadem
International Hospital**
Category: Hospital
Year: 2007
Client: APY
Architectural Planning: Sante
Architectural Office + Altay Erol
Electrical Planning: APY
Mechanical Planning: APY
Static Strengthening:
EQRM International

Farmatek
Category: Office
Year: 2008
Client: Hakan Yildirim
Architectural Planning:
MEDA Architecture
Electrical Planning: Ahmet Aksoy
Mechanical Planning: Selcuk Gurun
Static Engineers: Turgut Altinsoy

Dumankaya Modern Vadi Showroom
Category: Residential
Year: 2008
Client: Dumankaya
Architectural Planning: DBArchitects
Electrical Planning: Dumankaya
(only for the showroom)
Mechanical Planning: Dumankaya
(only for the showroom)
Static Engineers: Dumankaya
(only for the showroom)

Bakirkoy Acibadem Hospital
Category: Hospital

Year: 2008
Client: APY
Architectural Planning:
Tabanlioglu Architects
Electrical Planning: APY
Mechanical Planning: APY

Roche
Category: Office
Year: 2009
Client: Roche
Electrical Planning: ELS
Electrical Installation: ELS
Mechanical Planning: Ersa + Politerm
Mechanical Installation: Ersa + Politerm

Dumankaya Ikon Sales Office
Category: Residential
Year: 2009
Client: Dumankaya
Architectural Planning:
TAGO Architects
Electrical Planning: Dumankaya
(only for the sales office)
Mechanical Planning: Dumankaya
(only for the sales office)
Static Engineers: Dumankaya
(only for the sales office)

Maslak Acibadem Hospital
Category: Hospital
Year: 2009
Client: APY
Architectural Planning:
Ertunga Architectural Office
Electrical Planning: APY
Mechanical Planning: APY

Tiara Jewellery
Category: Retail
Year: 2010

Client: Garbis Atmaca
Architectural Planning:
Kemal Ahmet Aru

Atasehir Memorial Hospital
Category: Hospital
Year: 2010
Client: Memorial Health Group
Architectural Planning:
Memorial Project Coordinators

Intema Showroom Nisantasi
Category: Retail
Year: 2010
Client: Intema
Mechanical Installation: Politerm
Lighting: EA
Metal Work: 888 DESIGN
Plasterboard: Bayarlar Construction
Furniture: Akal Construction
Detail: Om Architectural Office + Ayrit

Kavacik Medistate Hospital
Category: Hospital
Year: 2010
Client: Medistate Health Group
Architectural Planning:
TAGO Architects

Aspen Fair Stand 2010
Category: Fair Stand
Year: 2010
Client: Aspen
Architectural Planning: Zoom/TPU
Electrical Installation: Akademi
Mechanical Installation: Akademi
Signboard: Panel Graphics

Sisli Memorial Hospital
Category: Hospital
Year: 2010

Client: Memorial Health Group
Architectural Planning:
Memorial Project Coordinators
Electrical Planning: Dasel
Mechanical Planning: Ersa

SALT Galata Auditorium
Category: Culture
Year: 2011
Client: SALT
Architectural Project:
Alexandre Vallaury
Renovation Project: Han Tumertekin
Electrical Planning: ENKOM
Mechanical Planning: Haluk Derya
Static Engineers: Celal Erdem
Sound System: Avitec

Henkel Showroom
Category: Retail
Year: 2011
Client: Henkel
Mechanical Planning:
MY Karasu
Static Engineers:
Global Investment Holdings

ER-PA Hospital
Category: Hospital
Year: 2011
Client: ER-PA
Architectural Planning:
Lina Architectural Office
Electrical Planning: Unal Sengun
Mechanical Planning: Seref Hazer
Static Engineers: Sait Yaymanoglu

Aspen Fair Stand 2011
Category: Fair Stand
Year: 2011
Client: Aspen
Architectural Planning: Zoom/TPU
Electrical Installation: Planet
Mechanical Installation: Planet
Construction: Aci
Signboard: Panel Graphics
Furniture: Akal Construction

**Istanbul Florence
Nightingale Hospital**
Category: Hospital
Year: 2012
Client: Group Florence Nightingale
Architectural Planning: Sevki Pekin
Electrical Planning: Omega
Mechanical Planning: Gurbey

Static Engineers: Irfan Balioglu

Urgan
Category: Office
Year: 2012
Client: Urgan
Architectural Planning: ART
Electrical Planning: Metraj
Electrical Installation: Metraj
Mechanical Planning: Cag Heating
Mechanical Installation: Cag Heating
Plasterboard and Paint: Kackar

Ulus Liv Hospital
Category: Hospital
Year: 2012
Client: FOMGRUP
Architectural Planning:
Tumay Architectural Office
Electrical Planning: FOMGRUP
Mechanical Planning: FOMGRUP

Zoom/TPU Office
Category: Office
Year: 2012
Client: Zoom/TPU
Architectural Planning: ART
Electrical Planning: Ank
Electrical Installation: Metraj
Mechanical Installation: Cag Heating
Plasterboard and Paint: Kackar

LOSEV Facility
Category: Hospital,
School, Hotel
Year: 2013–ongoing
Client: LOSEV
Architectural Planning:
Kreatif Architectural Office
Electrical Planning: HB Technics
Mechanical Planning: GMD Project
Static Engineers: Erduman
Landscape: ON Design
Infrastructure: Sigal

Ankara Memorial Hospital
Category: Hospital
Year: 2013
Client: Y. Y. Saglik
(Memorial Health Group)
Architectural Planning:
MSA Architectural Office
Electrical Planning: Cebirler
Mechanical Planning: Cebirler

TR-Pharm
Category: Office

Year: 2013
Client: TR-Pharm
Architectural Planning:
Tabanlioglu Architects
Electrical Planning: SIEMENS
Electrical Installation: EM Group
Mechanical Planning: DEMTA
Mechanical Installation: Cebirler
Decoration: Gulsan
Plasterboard and Paint: ENSAR
Furniture: BMS + NEOTEK
Lighting: Optimum

Zorlu Memorial Clinic
Category: Hospital
Year: 2013
Client: Memorial Health Group
Architectural Planning:
EAA Emre Arolat Architects
Electrical Planning:
Memorial Project Coordinators
Mechanical Planning:
Memorial Project Coordinators

Kolan Hospital
Category: Hospital
Year: 2013
Client: Kolan Health Group
Architectural Planning: Piramit
Electrical Planning: ERKP+Cebirler
Mechanical Planning: Birlesim+Cebirler

Ankara Liv Hospital
Category: Hospital
Year: 2014
Client: FOMGRUP
Architectural Planning:
Omer Camoglu
Electrical Planning: FOMGRUP
Mechanical Planning: FOMGRUP

Karakoy Hotel
Category: Hotel
Year: 2014
Client:
Bozlu Holding + International Group
Architectural Planning: Levon Nafilyan

Erciyes Hotel
Category: Hotel
Year: 2014
Client: Ali Kibar + Fatih Karamanci
Architectural Planning: Zoom/TPU

Avrasya Hospital
Category: Hospital

Year: 2015
Client: Urlu Saglik
Architectural Planning: Unay Mimarlik
Electrical Planning: Nevzat Ciftcioglu
Electrical Installation: Emas Elektrik
Mechanical Planning: Niyazi Yirmibes
Mechanical Installation:
Keskin Konsept Yapi
Static Engineers: Serkan Pekcan

Gentas Fair Stand
Category: Fair Stand
Year: 2015
Client: Gentas
Architectural Planning: Zoom/TPU
Electrical Planning: EM Group
Electrical Installation: EM Group
Mechanical Planning: Uluterm
Mechanical Installation: Uluterm
Static Engineers: 888 Design

Complete Project List

Project name	Year	Size	Type	Location
Derimod Antalya	1994	300 m²	Retail	Antalya
Derimod Bahariye	1994	200 m²	Retail	Istanbul
Derimod Caddebostan	1994	400 m²	Retail	Istanbul
Derimod Akmerkez	1994	90 m²	Retail	Istanbul
Aktar Alsancak	1994	180 m²	Retail	Izmir
Aktar Showroom Nisantasi	1994	182 m²	Retail	Istanbul
Naturland Foundations Kemer	1994	10,000 m²	Hotel	Antalya
Borusan Makina (Boatshow Fair)	1994	90 m²	Fair Stand	Istanbul
Borusan Makina (Izmir Fair)	1994	400 m²	Fair Stand	Izmir
Fine Line Osmanbey	1994	160 m²	Retail	Istanbul
Smyrne Dessert (Carrefour Shopping Mall) Kozyatagi	1995	43 m²	Restaurant	Istanbul
Carousel Shopping Mall Bakirkoy	1995	22,000 m²	Shopping Mall	Istanbul
Yargici Bahariye	1995	225 m²	Retail	Istanbul
YKM Sisli	1995	10,000 m²	Retail	Istanbul
EgeBank Main Branch	1995	2000 m²	Bank	Istanbul
Esrefoglu A.S. Central Office	1995	1000 m²	Office	Bursa
Eta A.S. Central Office Arrangement Altunizade	1995	1200 m²	Office	Istanbul
Marta Ltd. Sti. Showroom Balmumcu	1995	220 m²	Retail	Istanbul
Derimod Erenkoy	1995	150 m²	Retail	Istanbul
Aktar Osmanbey	1996	180 m²	Retail	Istanbul
Derimod (Carousel Shopping Mall) Bakirkoy	1996	184 m²	Retail	Istanbul
Derimod Nisantasi	1996	200 m²	Retail	Istanbul
Aktar Nisantasi	1996	120 m²	Retail	Istanbul
YKM (Gulfstar Shopping Mall)	1996	2200 m²	Retail	Izmit
YKM Antalya	1996	1700 m²	Retail	Antalya
Charactere Nisantasi	1996	225 m²	Retail	Istanbul
RoBank	1996	3000 m²	Bank	Bucharest, Romania

Project name	Year	Size	Type	Location
Alfateks A.S Showroom Nisantasi	1996	240 m²	Retail	Istanbul
Can Kurtaran Holding Ekosan Karakoy	1996	2000 m²	Office	Istanbul
YKM Head Office 4.Levent	1996	1000 m²	Office	Istanbul
Maya Jewellery (Intercontinental Hotel) Taksim	1997	60 m²	Retail	Istanbul
Istanbul Lutfi Kirdar ICEC Harbiye	1997	22,000 m²	Congress Center	Istanbul
Aktar Textile CNR Expo (1) Yesilkoy	1997	72 m²	Fair Stand	Istanbul
Aktar Textile CNR Expo (2) Yesilkoy	1997	68 m²	Fair Stand	Istanbul
Aktar Cekirge	1997	220 m²	Retail	Bursa
Aktar Suadiye	1997	202 m²	Retail	Istanbul
Adil Babies' Garment	1997	220 m²	Retail	Mersin
Adil Mersin	1997	237 m²	Retail	Mersin
Motivi (Galleria Shopping Mall) Atakoy	1997	140 m²	Retail	Istanbul
Motivi Suadiye	1997	140 m²	Retail	Istanbul
Motivi Nisantasi	1997	120 m²	Retail	Istanbul
YKM Suadiye	1997	5,200 m²	Retail	Istanbul
Manati Bahariye	1997	210 m²	Retail	Istanbul
Sevgi Hospital (Carousel Acibadem Hospital)	1997	6,200 m²	Hospital	Istanbul
Gizmo Showroom Okmeydani	1997	600 m²	Retail	Istanbul
Baytur Autoshow (Subaru stall) Yesilkoy	1997	200 m²	Fair Stand	Istanbul
Eksan Textile Office Merter	1997	3,000 m²	Office	Istanbul
YKM (Zafer Plaza)	1997	3,200 m²	Retail	Bursa
Schlotzky's Deli Restaurant Saskinbakkal	1997	150 m²	Restaurant	Istanbul
Smart Play Children's Club (Migros Shopping Mall) Beylikduzu	1998	250 m²	Facility	Istanbul
Migros Shopping Mall (part 1) Beylikduzu	1998	30,000 m²	Shopping Mall	Istanbul
Aktar (EGS Park Shopping Mall)	1998	140 m²	Retail	Izmir
Aktar Textile CNR Expo (3) Yesilkoy	1998	110 m²	Fair Stand	Istanbul
Adil	1998	400 m²	Retail	Mersin
Bind Chocolate Kiosk (Carrousel Shopping Mall) Bakirkoy	1998	12 m²	Retail	Istanbul
Italbi Cekirge	1998	200 m²	Retail	Bursa
TSE Quality Campus Cayirova	1998	5000 m²	Facility	Istanbul
Serifoglu Parquet Head Office and Showroom 4.Levent	1998	400 m²	Office+Retail	Istanbul
Serifoglu Parquet (YAPI-Turkeybuild) Beylikduzu	1998	48 m²	Fair Stand	Istanbul
Teba Beylikduzu	1998	400 m²	Fair Stand	Istanbul
Migros Shopping Mall (part 2) Beylikduzu	1998	15,000 m²	Shopping Mall	Istanbul
Smart Play Migros Ankara	1998	300 m²	Retail	Ankara
Schlotzky's Deli Restaurant Caddebostan	1999	500 m²	Restaurant	Istanbul
Zafer Plaza Shopping Mall	1999	70,000 m²	Shopping Mall	Bursa
Derimod (Zafer Plaza)	1999	240 m²	Retail	Bursa
Derimod (Migros Shopping Mall)	1999	140 m²	Retail	Ankara
Yargici (Profilo Shopping Mall) Mecidiyekoy	1999	120 m²	Retail	Istanbul
Aktar (Migros Shopping Mall)	1999	200 m²	Retail	Ankara
Aktar (Mavisehir Shopping Mall)	1999	150 m²	Retail	Izmir
Inci (Zafer Plaza)	1999	140 m²	Retail	Bursa

Project name	Year	Size	Type	Location
Inci Saskinbakkal	1999	150 m²	Retail	Istanbul
Inci (Migros Shopping Mall)	1999	180 m²	Retail	Ankara
YKM Kids Section Sisli	1999	450 m²	Retail	Istanbul
YKM Perfumery Department Sisli	1999	1000 m²	Retail	Istanbul
Koc University Auditorium Kilyos	1999	2500 m²	Auditorium	Istanbul
Rotta Corp. Co Kozyatagi	1999	450 m²	Retail	Istanbul
Cihangir Leather Ikitelli	1999	280 m²	Retail	Istanbul
Schlotzky's Deli Restaurant (Istiklal Street) Taksim	1999	320 m²	Restaurant	Istanbul
Migros Supermarket Kiosk Design (Migros Shopping Mall)	1999	2000 m²	Retail	Ankara
Derimod Kavaklidere	1999	400 m²	Retail	Ankara
Motivi Adana	1999	260 m²	Retail	Adana
Inci Central Office Topkapi	1999	4000 m²	Office	Istanbul
Schlotzsky's Deli Restaurant Mecidiyekoy	2000	300 m²	Restaurant	Istanbul
Schlotzsky's Deli Restaurant Akmerkez	2000	280 m²	Restaurant	Istanbul
Cafe MIO Tesvikiye	2000	120 m²	Restaurant	Istanbul
Ceni and Vedat Dekohen Residence Ortakoy	2000	400 m²	Residential	Istanbul
Resadiye Houses Resadiye	2000	450 m²	Residential	Istanbul
YKM Konak	2000	7000 m²	Retail	Izmir
YKM (Real Shopping Mall)	2000	2200 m²	Retail	Izmir
YKM (Karadeniz Ereglisi)	2000	750 m²	Retail	Zonguldak
YKM Adana	2000	4800 m²	Retail	Adana
YKM (Carrefour Shopping Mall)	2000	5000 m²	Retail	Izmit
YKM (Galleria Shopping Mall) Atakoy	2000	10,800 m²	Retail	Istanbul
YKM Afyon	2000	3000 m²	Retail	Afyon
YKM Mersin	2000	5000 m²	Retail	Mersin
Istanbul Lutfi Kirdar ICEC Harbiye (2nd division)	2000	6000 m²	Congress Center	Istanbul
ATK Tekstil Yesilkoy	2000	270 m²	Retail	Istanbul
Yesim Teks Tarabya	2000	600 m²	Retail	Istanbul
Figen and Servet Yazici Residence	2001	1300 m²	Residential	Antalya
Praktiker (Carrefour Shopping Mall) Mavisehir	2001	500 m²	Retail	Izmir
YKM 4.Levent	2001	2440 m²	Retail	Istanbul
Zara (Migros Shopping Mall)	2001	2000 m²	Retail	Antalya
Lotus Hotel Kemer	2001	12,000 m²	Hotel	Antalya
Sheraton Hotel Kirkuk	2001	25,000 m²	Hotel	Kirkuk, Iraq
Rahsan Saruhan Tan Houses Suadiye	2001	280 m²	Residential	Istanbul
SushiCo Chinese in Town Nisantasi	2002	350 m²	Restaurant	Istanbul
Nike Bilkent	2002	40 m²	Retail	Ankara
Nike Trabzon	2002	150 m²	Retail	Trabzon
Nike (Galleria Shopping Mall) Atakoy	2002	180 m²	Retail	Istanbul
Nike (Carrefour Shopping Mall) Kozyatagi	2002	90 m²	Retail	Istanbul
Nike (Carousel Shopping Mall) Bakirkoy	2002	130 m²	Retail	Istanbul
Nike (Armada Shopping Mall) Sogutozu	2002	150 m²	Retail	Ankara
Nike (Nautilus Shopping Mall) Kosuyolu	2002	220 m²	Retail	Istanbul
Nike Play (Akmerkez Shopping Mall) Etiler	2002	50 m²	Retail	Istanbul

Project name	Year	Size	Type	Location
Zara (Akmerkez Shopping Mall) Etiler	2002	1050 m²	Retail	Istanbul
Zara Suadiye	2002	2500 m²	Retail	Istanbul
YKM Saskinbakkal	2002	800 m²	Retail	Istanbul
HOSIM	2002	35,000 m²	Retail	Istanbul
Sutluce Cultural Center	2002	85,000 m²	Facility	Istanbul
Royal Motors Auto Gallery Etiler	2002	190 m²	Auto Gallery	Istanbul
Bessini Beylikduzu	2002	1200 m²	Retail	Istanbul
Bessini Suadiye	2003	120 m²	Retail	Istanbul
Babos Cark Caddesi	2003	630 m²	Retail	Adapazari
Sumer Jewelry Storks	2003	6000 m²	Retail	Antalya
Bank Europa Nisantasi Branch	2003	500 m²	Bank	Istanbul
Bank Europa Suadiye Branch	2003	250 m²	Bank	Istanbul
Bank Europa Etiler Branch	2003	225 m²	Bank	Istanbul
Bank Europa Levent Branch	2003	200 m²	Bank	Istanbul
Bank Europa Altunizade Branch	2003	240 m²	Bank	Istanbul
Bank Europa Saskinbakkal Branch	2003	210 m²	Bank	Istanbul
Bank Europa Yesilkoy Branch	2003	240 m²	Bank	Istanbul
Abt Tekstil Yesilkoy	2003	300 m²	Retail	Istanbul
Nike Beyoglu	2003	1500 m²	Retail	Istanbul
Acibadem Clinic	2004	2800 m²	Hospital	Istanbul
Bank Europa Maslak Branch	2004	280 m²	Bank	Istanbul
Bank Europa Yenikoy Branch	2004	430 m²	Bank	Istanbul
Bank Europa Alsancak Branch	2004	230 m²	Bank	Izmir
Gate Gourmet Usas (Port Lara Beach)	2004	20,000 m²	Restaurant	Antalya
Gebe (Is Bankasi Bloklari) Levent	2005	40 m²	Retail	Istanbul
Acibadem CNR Expo Yesilkoy	2005	30 m²	Fair Stand	Istanbul
Kadikoy Florence Nightingale Hospital	2005	7532 m²	Hospital	Istanbul
Varan Bus Company Gumussuyu Branch	2005	220 m²	Facility	Istanbul
Vakko Akmerkez Etiler	2005	570 m²	Retail	Istanbul
Bursa Acibadem Hospital	2006	28,500 m²	Hospital	Bursa
Presidential Residence	2006	1500 m²	Residential	Astana, Kazakhstan
Pierre Cardin Osmanbey	2006	400 m²	Retail	Istanbul
Pierre Cardin (Nautilus Shopping Mall) Kadikoy	2006	130 m²	Retail	Istanbul
Pierre Cardin Kayseri	2006	165 m²	Retail	Kayseri
Pierre Cardin Bornova	2006	170 m²	Retail	Izmir
Pierre Cardin Izmir	2006	202 m²	Retail	Izmir
Pierre Cardin Beylikduzu	2006	240 m²	Retail	Istanbul
Pierre Cardin Bornova	2006	291 m²	Retail	Izmir
Pierre Cardin Samsun	2006	330 m²	Retail	Samsun
Pierre Cardin Bahcesehir	2006	232 m²	Retail	Istanbul
Pierre Cardin Kizilay	2006	400 m²	Retail	Ankara
Pierre Cardin Adana	2006	170 m²	Retail	Adana
Pierre Cardin Baku	2006	170 m²	Retail	Baku, Azerbaijan
Pierre Cardin – Moscow Fair Stand	2006	184 m²	Fair Stand	Moscow, Russia
Pierre Cardin – Zuchex Fair Stand	2006	63 m²	Fair Stand	Baku, Azerbaijan
Darty (Istinye Park Shopping Mall)	2006	1150 m²	Retail	Istanbul

Project name	Year	Size	Type	Location
Darty (Profilo Shopping Mall) Mecidiyekoy	2006	1350 m²	Retail	Istanbul
Afrodit Exclusive	2006	120 m²	Retail	Istanbul
Bessini Nisantasi	2006	350 m²	Retail	Istanbul
Kadikoy Acibadem Hospital	2006	42,000 m²	Hospital	Istanbul
Acibadem Contact Office Bilecik	2006	110 m²	Office	Bilecik
Acibadem Contact Office Bolu	2006	150 m²	Office	Bolu
Acibadem Contact Office Tekirdag	2006	30 m²	Office	Tekirdag
Acibadem Contact Office Yalova	2006	140 m²	Office	Yalova
Acibadem Contact Office Adapazari	2006	135 m²	Office	Adapazari
Acibadem Contact Office Balikesir	2006	100 m²	Office	Balikesir
Acibadem Contact Office Canakkale	2006	120 m²	Office	Canakkale
Izmit Acibadem Hospital	2006	5000 m²	Hospital	Izmit
Beylikduzu Acibadem	2006	2650 m²	Hospital	Istanbul
Kısıkli Acibadem Labmed Medical Laboratory	2006	1200 m²	Hospital	Istanbul
Mahmut Serbes Jewellery	2006	215 m²	Retail	Adapazari
Darty (Kale Shopping Mall) Gungoren	2007	1000 m²	Retail	Istanbul
Darty Koctas Yenibosna	2007	5400 m²	Retail	Istanbul
Darty Head Office Elmadag	2007	850 m²	Office	Istanbul
Darty (Markiz Arcade)	2007	1480 m²	Retail	Istanbul
Darty (Profilo Shopping Mall) Mecidiyekoy	2007	1350 m²	Retail	Istanbul
Darty (Carousel Shopping Mall) Bakirkoy	2007	1450 m²	Retail	Istanbul
Derimod Ankara	2007	150 m²	Retail	Ankara
Derimod (Istinye Park Shopping Mall)	2007	120 m²	Retail	Istanbul
Derimod Capacity	2007	240 m²	Retail	Istanbul
Jimer Hospital	2007	12,000 m²	Hospital	Bursa
Yesilkoy Acibadem International Hospital	2007	20,000 m²	Hospital	Istanbul
Continuum	2008	100 m²	Retail	Istanbul
Bakirkoy Acibadem Hospital	2008	17,500 m²	Hospital	Istanbul
Kucukcekmece Dogan Hospital	2008	2500 m²	Hospital	Istanbul
Farmatek	2008	2200 m²	Office	Istanbul
Dumankaya Ikon Residences	2008	95 m²	Residential	Istanbul
Dumankaya Modern Vadi Showroom	2008	1200 m²	Residential	Istanbul
Tesco Kipa	2008	35,000 m²	Retail	Yalova
Tunnel Residences	2008	2000 m²	Residential	Istanbul
Goynuk Spa and Center Hotel	2008	30,000 m²	Hotel	Bolu
Maslak Acibadem Hospital	2009	40,000 m²	Hospital	Istanbul
Adana Acibadem Hospital	2009	15,000 m²	Hospital	Adana
Kayseri Acibadem Hospital	2009	20,000 m²	Hospital	Kayseri
Atasehir Acibadem	2009	7050 m²	Hospital	Istanbul
Fulya Acibadem Hospital	2009	20,100 m²	Hospital	Istanbul
Eskisehir Acibadem Hospital	2009	20,000 m²	Hospital	Ekisehir
Roche	2009	6000 m²	Office	Istanbul
Teva Head Office Maslak	2009	1200 m²	Office	Istanbul
Almana Ford Auto Showroom 2 (conceptual design)	2009	60,000 m²	Auto Gallery	Doha, Qatar
Almana Ford Auto Showroom 1 (conceptual design)	2009	27,000 m²	Auto Gallery	Doha, Qatar

Project name	Year	Syze	Type	Location
Dumankaya Gizli Bahce Villas	2009	300 m²	Residential	Istanbul
Dumankaya Ikon Sales Office	2009	400 m²	Residential	Istanbul
Kavacik Medistate Hospital	2010	15,000 m²	Hospital	Istanbul
Roche Head Office	2010	800 m²	Office	Istanbul
Pfizer	2010	9000 m²	Office	Istanbul
Atasehir Memorial Hospital	2010	5000 m²	Hospital	Istanbul
Sirte Seaside Hotel	2010	20,330 m²	Hotel	Sirte, Libya
Italian Restaurant	2010	1100 m²	Restaurant	Tripoli, Libya
Aspen Fair Stand 2010	2010	120 m²	Fair Stand	Istanbul
Sisli Memorial Hospital	2010	30,000 m²	Hospital	Istanbul
Antalya Memorial Hospital	2010	10,000 m²	Hospital	Antalya
Tiara Jewellery	2010	300 m²	Retail	Istanbul
Dumankaya Kurtkoy Trend Showroom	2010	555 m²	Residential	Istanbul
Intema Showroom Nisantasi	2010	213 m²	Retail	Istanbul
Intema Showroom Izmir	2010	280 m²	Retail	Izmir
Intema Showroom Ankara	2010	350 m²	Retail	Ankara
Best Buy Ankara	2010	3000 m²	Retail	Ankara
Private Villa	2011	1880 m²	Residential	Le Pont-de-Montvert, France
Dumankaya Vizyon Pendik Lobbies	2011	1265 m²	Residential	Istanbul
Aspen Fair Stand 2011	2011	120 m²	Fair Stand	Istanbul
Samsun Medicana Hospital	2011	28,000 m²	Hospital	Samsun
SALT Galata Auditorium	2011	330 m²	Culture	Istanbul
Henkel Showroom	2011	538 m²	Retail	Istanbul
ER-PA Hospital	2011	26,600 m²	Hospital	Denizli
Bagcilar Medipol Mega Hospital	2011	46,000 m²	Hospital	Istanbul
Faruk Medical Center	2012	44,000 m²	Hospital	Sulaymaniyah, Iraq
BYZ Shopping Mall	2012	16,507 m²	Shopping Mall	Kayseri
Urgan	2012	2000 m²	Office	Istanbul
Zoom/TPU Office	2012	300 m²	Office	Istanbul
Istanbul Florence Nightingale Hospital	2012	56,000 m²	Hospital	Istanbul
Ulus Liv Hospital	2012	27,987 m²	Hospital	Istanbul
Ankara Memorial Hospital	2013	30,989 m²	Hospital	Ankara
Almana Residence Kavacik	2013	600 m²	Residential	Istanbul
Dumankaya Ikon (common areas)	2013	1500 m²	Residential	Istanbul
Dentway Dent Clinic	2013	270 m²	Hospital	Istanbul
Kolan Hospital	2013	18,652 m²	Hospital	Istanbul
Bayrampasa Kolan Hospital	2013	7940 m²	Hospital	Istanbul
LOSEV Facility	2013	130,000 m²	Multipurpose	Ankara
TR-Pharm	2013	587 m²	Office	Istanbul
Zorlu Memorial Clinic	2013	255 m²	Hospital	Istanbul
Sinerji	2014	230 m²	Office	Baku, Azerbaijan
Ankara Liv Hosital	2014	15,000 m²	Hospital	Ankara
Karakoy Hotel	2014	2400 m²	Hotel	Istanbul
Erciyes Hotel	2014	10,000 m²	Hotel	Kayseri
Avrasya Hospital	2014	30,000 m²	Hospital	Istanbul
Gentas Fair Stand	2015	280 m²	Fair Stand	Istanbul

Awards

1987
Sedat Gurel Dalyankoy Museum
and Library Competition,
2nd Place (Levent Cirpici)

1998
Serifoglu Parkett Fair Stand
21st YAPI-Turkeybuild Awards,
"Best Stand Design Serving Its
Purpose", 2nd Prize

1999
Taklamakan Bench
IFDA (International Furniture Design
Fair Asahikawa, Japan), shortlist
(Atilla Kuzu)

2001
Figen and Servet Yazici Residence
Nominated for the Aga Khan Award
for Architecture

2002
**From Alaska to
Barringer Coffee Table**
IFDA (International Furniture Design
Fair Asahikawa, Japan), shortlist
(Atilla Kuzu)

2005
Acibadem Clinic
Design Turkey, Interior Design Award
by art+deco, "Public Space", 1st Prize

2009
Maslak Acibadem Hospital
WAF (World Architecture Festival),
Barcelona, Spain, shortlist

2010
Angle Table
Design Turkey, Best Design Award,
"Home Furniture" (Atilla Kuzu)

2010
Elle Decor International Design
Awards, Turkey, "Designer of the
Year" (Atilla Kuzu)

2010
Open Kitchen
Elle Decor International Design
Awards, Turkey, "Best Kitchen
Design" (Atilla Kuzu)

2010
Best Solution Partner Award,
Dumankaya Construction, Turkey,
1st Prize

2010
Aspen Fair Stand 2010
33rd YAPI-Turkeybuild Awards, "Best
Stand Design Serving Its Purpose",
1st Prize

2011
Aspen Fair Stand 2011
34th YAPI-Turkeybuild, Altin Miknatis
Awards, "Best Stand Design",
1st Prize

2011
Ulus Liv Hospital
WAF (World Architecture Festival),
Barcelona, Spain, shortlist

2012
Fluido Kitchen
Elle Decor International
Design Awards, Turkey, "Kitchen",
1st Prize (Atilla Kuzu)

2014
**Istanbul Florence
Nightingale Hospital**
Sign of the City, Turkey,
"Best Healthcare Project"

2015
Gentas Fair Stand 2015
38th YAPI-Turkeybuild, Altin Miknatis
Awards, "Best Stand Design",
1st Prize

Acknowledgements

We would like to espress our thanks to our dear Funda Cakir Mehter, who has been with us from the very beginninng of this book project and who has managed the process and organization successfully. To Philip Jodidio, for being the author of the book, for his contribution to the general coordination of the project and for his essay. To Celal Abdi Guzer, for triggering this book idea and supporting us with his insightful contribution. And many thanks to the designer of the book Thomas Manss and the Prestel team of Katharina Haderer and Constanze Holler. Our thanks also to the copy editor of the book Harriet Graham, for being so patient and understanding again and again.

To our beloved families for being with us, supporting us along the entire journey while we have been accomplishing these projects. To all recent and former team members of Zoom/TPU for their tireless efforts.

To all employers and employee representatives for their trust and support.

To all collaborators who have been listed below, we are always thankful to all and we send you our greetings and love.

Atilla Kuzu + Levent Cirpici, Istanbul, Turkey, 2015

Suat Gizem Akgun, Alper Tolga Arıkan, Umur Arsoy, Guzide Aslankaya, Erman Aycan, Pinar Baytekin, Ata Benli, Ozge Berberoglu, Isil Gonul Budak, Uygur Bulut, Umit Caglar, Seda Camgoz, Ceren Celikel, Selen Baskan Collange, Nihan Dedeoglu, Ulku Demir, Esra Demiray, Esin Ekinci, Mehmet Erciyes, Bilge Eryilmaz, Alp Germaner, Adem Gul, Melis Guler, Selami Gunduzeri, Zeynep Inanc, Fatma Kalic, Melih Kanbur, Yunus Emre Kara, Suda Karaduman, Mertcan Karakus, Sebnem Keskin, Pinar Kocaman, Gokce Koparal, Makbule Secil Korkmaz, Gulnur Mimir, Irem Mucur, Begum Oncul, Dincer Orhan, Aygen Taskiran Ozdemir, Bulent Ozden, Serkan Ozkan, Sadik Pohrenk, Jakub Kosma Poplawski, Ekin Naz Samiloglu, Sibel Sanlav, Sinemis Sarigul Kara, Ozgun Sengew, Karani Soysert, Fernaz Tagvimi, Ozgen Taskiran, Banu Tomruk, Mustafa Turanli, Ozge Ugur, Jeyan Ulku, Deniz Uner, Mahmut Yildiz, Selami Yilmaz

Imprint

© Prestel Verlag
Munich · London · New York 2015

Front Cover: Zorlu Memorial Clinic

Prestel Verlag, Munich
A member of Verlagsgruppe
Random House GmbH

Prestel Verlag
Neumarkter Strasse 28
81673 Munich
Tel. +49 (0)89 4136-0
Fax +49 (0)89 4136-2335

www.prestel.de

Prestel Publishing Ltd.
14-17 Wells Street
London W1T 3PD
Tel. +44 (0)20 7323-5004
Fax +44 (0)20 7323-0271

Prestel Publishing
900 Broadway, Suite 603
New York, NY 10003
Tel. +1 (212) 995-2720
Fax +1 (212) 995-2733

www.prestel.com

Library of Congress Control
Number is available; British Library
Cataloguing-in-Publication Data:
a catalogue record for this book is
available from the British Library;
Deutsche Nationalbibliothek holds
a record of this publication in the
Deutsche Nationalbibliografie;
detailed bibliographical data can
be found under: http://www.dnb.de

Project coordination:
Funda Cakir Mehter
Editorial direction Prestel:
Constanze Holler
Copyediting: Harriet Graham
Photographers: Murat Alpguven,
Ali Bekman, Cemal Emdem,
Ege Turkmenler, Busra Yeltekin
Design and layout:
Thomas Manss & Company
Production: Andrea Cobré
Origination: Royalmedia, Munich
Printing and binding:
Passavia, Passau

Typeface: Benton Sans
Paper: 150g Hello silk

All the designs on pages introducing
new sections in the book are the
work of Zoom/TPU.

Printed in Germany

ISBN 978-3-7913-5441-5

Verlagsgruppe Random House
FSC® N001967
printed on the
FSC®-certified paper Hello silk